G000165784

HIGI

CREDIT SCORE

SECRETS

The Smart Raise and Repair Guide to Excellent Credit

Revision 1.74

Thomas Herold

highcreditscoresecrets.com

Table of Contents

Copyright & Disclaimer

be liable for any loss of profit or any other commercial damage, including but not limited to special, incidental, consequential, or other damages.

This book is presented solely for educational and entertainment purposes. The author and publisher are not offering it as legal, accounting, or other professional services advice. While best efforts have been used in preparing this book, the author and publisher make no representations or warranties of any kind and assume no liabilities of any kind with respect to the accuracy or completeness of the contents and specifically disclaim any implied warranties of merchantability or fitness of use for a particular purpose.

The information and/or documents contained in this book do not constitute legal or financial advice and should never be used without first consulting with a financial professional to determine what may be best for your individual needs.

The publisher and the author do not make any guarantee or other promise as to any results that may be obtained from using the content of this book. You should never make any investment decision without first consulting with your own financial advisor and conducting your own research and due diligence. To the maximum extent permitted by law, the publisher and the author disclaim any and all liability in the event any information, commentary, analysis, opinions, advice and/or recommendations contained in this book prove to be inaccurate, incomplete or unreliable, or result in any investment or other losses.

Content contained or made available through this book is not intended to and does not constitute legal advice or investment advice and no attorney-client relationship is formed.

The publisher and the author are providing this book and its contents on an "as is" basis. Your use of the information in this book is at your own risk.

Neither the author nor the publisher shall be held liable or responsible to any person or entity with respect to any loss or incidental or consequential damages caused, or alleged to have been caused, directly or indirectly, by the information or programs contained herein.

No warranty may be created or extended by sales representatives or written sales materials. Every company is different and the advice and strategies contained herein may not be suitable for your situation. You should seek the services of a competent professional before beginning any improvement program. The story and its characters and entities are fictional. Any likeness to actual persons, either living or dead, is strictly coincidental.

About the Author

Thomas Herold is a successful entrepreneur, mediator, author, and personal development coach. He published 36 books with over 200,000 copies distributed worldwide and is the founder of seven online businesses.

He is the founder and CEO of the 'Financial Terms Dictionary' book series and website, which explains in detail and comprehensive form over 1000 financial terms. In his financial book series, he informs in detail and with practical examples all aspects of the financial sector. His educational materials are designed to help people get started with financial education.

In his 2018 released book 'The Money Deception', Mr. Herold provides the most sophisticated insight and shocking details about the current monetary system. Never before has the massive manipulation of money caused so much economic inequality in the world. In spite of these frightening facts, 'The Money Deception' also provides remarkable and simple solutions to create abundance for all people, and it's a must-read to survive the global monetary transformation that's underway right now.

In 2019 Thomas Herold released an entirely new financial book series explaining in detail and with practical examples financial terms. The 'Herold Financial IQ Series' includes 16 titles, covering every aspect and category of the financial market.

Starting with Personal Finance, Real Estate and Banking term. Covering Corporate Finance, Investment as well as Economics. Also includes Retirement, Trading, and Accounting terms. In addition, you'll find Debt, Bankruptcy, Mortgage, Small Business, and Wall Street terminology explained. Not to forget Laws & Regulations as well as important acronyms and abbreviations.

For More Information Please Visit the Author's Websites:

High Credit Score Secrets – Ask Your Credit Question
highcreditscoresecrets.com

The Herold Financial Dictionary - Over 1000 Financial Terms Explained
financial-dictionary.info

The Herold Financial IQ Series - Financial Education Is Your Best Investment
financial-dictionary.com

The Money Deception - What Banks & Government Don't Want You to Know
moneydeception.com

The Author's Personal Credit Experience

Born and raised in Germany, I arrived 1989 in Hawaii for my overdue vacation, before working 3 years straight to build my second business. Seeing all these palm trees and beautiful sandy beaches was mind blowing to me. After coming back to Germany, I decided to sell my business and migrate to Hawaii.

Credit cards are not very common in Germany, at least not for the majority - the middle class. If people have credit cards they are connected to their bank account, and the due bill is automatically deducted each month from their main account. This means no extra credit, just another payment option.

For the first few years I did not care much for credit cards. I settled my bills with the usual checks, and that was it. If I did not have enough money I would go out and earn it first, and then spend it. Getting credit and spending it before earning it was not a possibility in my mind!

The day I visited another island, wanting to rent a car for a week, showed me the limitations of not having a credit card. No credit card - no car rental - just like that. That's when I got my first $500 credit card from Capital One.

A few years later (I don't remember the circumstances anymore), my life turn upside down, and I was desperately looking for cash to survive. I used the $500 on my Capital One card and did not pay it back for at least one year. I ignored the letters that came - I guess I felt ashamed - and I did not want to face the facts.

Well, you may know how it goes. In the end I had to pay back over $2100 to settle for this little piece of plastic. That is four times the amount that I had borrowed - what a hard lesson to learn!

Very upset about this, I dedicated never again to use any credit cards in my life. But as you probably know from your own experience, those decisions don't last very long. At one point you realize that every financial decision you make involves credit somehow. I also did not realize how my lack of credit would affect my cell phone contract, my car leasing costs, and years later my mortgage payments.

To make a long story short, several years later, I decided to start building credit again. The Capital One card was the only piece of plastic I could get with my current credit score. I used it for several months, purchased little things and paid it off every month on time. After six months, I asked for an increase in credit limit and was instantly approved for $1000. It was a revelation to me because I was rewarded for good financial behavior.

The "game" started to work in my favor now. The next step was to get a credit card issued by my own bank. I had already opened a checking and a savings account and both were in good standing. My bank approved this credit card, but told me that I had to guarantee it for a while with money from my checking account for security purpose. For this second credit card I was approved for $1000, which was raised after eight months to $2000 and then the security deposit was returned to me.

At that time I still had no idea about my own credit score and what a credit report was. I did not want to spend money on obtaining credit reports, and I was also very suspicious about these credit bureaus. To me, they had the same status as the court or the IRS. Just thinking about them gave me the sweats.

Finally, I began devouring financial books and started to feel more at ease around this hot topic. I gained more financial know-how, and I then felt more confident with my financial choices. The rules of this "credit game" started to make more sense to me as I was rewarded with more credit card offers in the mail. Picking up the next card, I charged items on it, and then paid it off at the end of the month.

More and better credit card offers arrived in my mailbox. I made sure not to apply for credit cards that came with yearly fees - just the ones that were offered free forever. After three years passed, I owned eight different credit cards with a combined $58,000 in total available credit.

My credit score was now at 798 - mission accomplished! Please understand - this does not mean that I had $58.000 to spend on a shopping spree! This amount just indicates how much the financial system trusts you. It also means that with a close to 800 score, you now can play a much better financial game.

For example, with a credit score of around 680, the first attempt to lease a car was extraordinarily difficult. It took a long time to negotiate the monthly payment plan of around $270 per month. Years later with a score of close to 800 I was getting a nice electric car for only $190 per month. The car dealer told me that bringing my payment under $200 was a result of my good credit score.

What I didn't know at this point was how important this financial foundation was for my upcoming investment experience. In 2002, I learned from reading various financial books how crucial it was to put money away (in savings) before anything else was paid. This very important step led to my first $5,000 savings in the bank. After reading through more (sometimes very confusing) investment books, and also by understanding the global monetary system, I decided to invest in commodities, especially in silver.

I do not want to go into too much detail, however, because of my good credit standing I was able to leverage my silver investment (through borrowing with the banks) by the factor of four! This meant that for every dollar that the silver price increased, I was making four dollars in profit. In 2008, shortly before the Global Financial Crisis, I had managed to grow my portfolio to almost half a million dollars. Most of that money I lost after the crash, but that is irrelevant for getting my point across.

It would have not possible without a good credit score.

I mention this for only one reason. You never know how your life will unfold, and what financial transactions you may become involved in. I never ever thought I would invest money in commodities, lease a car, or buy a home.

A *good credit score is the foundation to building almost everything!*

Introduction

Credit has become a gatekeeper for so many different things in American life. Consider these questions: Do you have bad credit? Is this bad credit stopping you from purchasing a house? Could it be keeping you from getting financing for a car? Are you struggling with paying your bills because of higher interest rates?

Are charge-offs, bankruptcies, repos, short-sales, judgments, late payments, collection accounts, and loan modifications stopping you from living the life you should have? These are some of the common problems that poor credit can cause you.

Estimates reveal that more than 80 million Americans suffer through their days with bad credit.

Imagine if you were able to get pre-qualified to buy the home you always wanted or the car you desire. What if you could be approved for a credit card or loan with the best available interest rates? There is no reason to allow bad credit to stop you from enjoying the life that you should.

The key to getting past these problems is to realize that your credit score impacts all of the choices that you will make in the future.

To give you a simple example of how much effect it has on your savings, consider a mortgage payment that differs in interest payments by just 2% (based on a lower and higher credit score). Let us assume that the sticker price of an average house is $300,000. You would make a down payment of 10%, leaving an amount financed by the bank of $270.000.

Now, we will first assume an interest rate on this mortgage of 5%, which amounts to a payment of $1,125 per month. That is based on a low credit score. With a better credit score, you may get a 3% mortgage, which includes a payment of $675 per month. That is a difference of $450 per month, which increases to $5,400 per year.

Given a 20 year mortgage payment plan, your credit score will cost you $108,000 in this real life example!

Another example may bring your financial experience even more home. Increasing your credit score from Good to Excellent saves you $43,100 over a lifetime. It gets even more obvious if you increase your score from 'fair' to "good", which will save you $86,200 over a lifetime. Your biggest financial advantage occurs when you increase your score from Poor to Fair, which will save you an incredible $158,700 over a lifetime! These examples are based on an average person who is around 37 years old and is living in California[1].

Image what else you could buy with that money. Even more important - imagine what you could earn in additional income if you would invest that money!

With tens of millions of Americans desperately needing assistance with credit repair, one of the biggest problems is the overall population's lack of knowledge of the credit industry and how it works.

Consider that the average young adult's credit score is approximately 630 while the ideal credit score is about 760.

You can see that there is a significant discrepancy between where most young adults are and where they need to be with their scores. Remember that you need a healthy credit score to live a happy financial life.

In this book you will understand the straightforward step by step process that professionals use to remove all negative items from your various credit reports. They can often delete late payments, judgments, collections, repos, liens, and bankruptcies. Here you will learn the strategies and methods that the major credit bureaus do not want you to know.

By employing the methods perfected by certified credit repair specialists and credit attorneys, you can successfully repair your personal credit.

This will not only impact the interest rate you pay on loans and debt but also the security deposits that you pay when making investments.

In this book you will gain a comprehensive understanding of the ways to remove unverifiable, inaccurate, and questionable judgments, charge-offs, and collections from your credit reports.

I will show you how to use simple to duplicate strategies to put a stop to harassment from debt collectors. You will learn step by step instructions for improving your credit score and the step by step process for settling your debts even if the debt collector does not wish to settle.

I also provide you with clear instructions on what you should do if the credit bureaus will not remove questionable, unverifiable, or inaccurate information. The book will go through recently passed reforms (that benefit consumers) in credit bureau practices, credit score calculation, and lending - and how you can take advantage of these.

Get ready for relevant and current information that is appropriate for the economic conditions of today. Prepare for this one step at a time game plan to rebuild your credit.

To keep this book up to date with the current financial laws and regulations, I have consulted with a financial specialist. At the moment of publication, this writing is all information that is both accurate and complies with current law and regulations. However, regulations can change quickly, and in the rare case that you find any incorrect information, please inform the author immediately by going on his website.

https://highcreditscoresecrets.com/contact/

Please consult with a financial professional before making any important financial decision!

Overview of the Chapters

The chapters in this book are arranged to support an easy learning sequence, which allows you to get slowly familiar with each topic. With each chapter we will dig deeper and get into the nuts and bolts.

Chapter 1 starts with answers to the most important and most common questions like which credit card is the best one, and should you go into debt to build up credit. This will help you to understand the important first decisions in building up new credit.

In chapter 2, you will get a good insight into the many benefits you gain from having good credit. Some of them may surprise you! In chapter 3 we go through all of the components that make up a credit score as well as how credit cards work in practice. Followed by chapter 4, which gives you a quick overview of where you stand with your score based on various facts like age and location.

With chapter 5 we look at different best practices for positively impacting your credit score. This involves taking active steps that will improve your credit. We will also look at the different kinds of loans and credit cards, and how they impact your score.

Chapter 6 looks at choices and decisions that negatively impact your credit score and how you can avoid these. Following by chapter 7, which goes through the nuts and bolts of what a credit report is and how you can monitor it.

In chapter 8 we take a more detailed look at the various information components contained in your credit report. With chapter 9 we consider the many specific steps you can take to build up credit using credit cards. This includes a look at the differences between good and bad debts.

In chapter 10 you will learn the most sensible credit practices - wherever you are in your personal and professional life.

Chapter 11 looks at specific steps that you can take to improve your credit both instantly and over the longer term. With chapter 12 we consider the steps you can take to repair your credit score on your own without using a company or lawyer

Chapter 13 looks at the various improvements a credit repair service can make to your credit history. This includes specific elements that that they can have removed and deleted from your credit file with the bureaus.

In the last chapter 14, we go through how you can hold on to your good credit (and credit score) and defend it against the many threats like identity fraud and theft.

Let's get started by taking a look at the most common questions and answers regarding personal credit!

Quick Answers & Solutions to the Most Common Questions

How Do Credit Cards Work?

The Consumer Point of View

From a consumer point of view (your viewpoint), credit cards are simply cards made out of plastic that permit you to access a credit card issuer's credit limit that they have provided to you.

This credit line works something like a loan.

A main difference is that the creditor does not deliver you the entire cash amount upfront. Instead the bank permits you to draw the credit amount that you wish to when you need it (on demand). They also let you use the "loan" again and again, so long as you repay the amount that you have borrowed.

This is why credit cards are often referred to as revolving accounts.

Every time that you buy something with your credit card, your available amount of credit decreases by this corresponding amount. Consider an example. If you have a $200 credit limit and you buy something for $50, then you will have $150 in remaining available credit. You owe your creditor (the bank) $50. You might charge something else for another $50 before your monthly statement arrives. In this case, you would owe the bank $100 and still have another $100 in remaining available credit.

What separates these credit cards from traditional loans is that you will again have access to your credit limit each time that you pay the balance down on this card. In the previous example, if you repaid the $100 total balance you had charged, you would then have $200 of available credit to use again.

It means that you can continuously spend as much as your available credit limit and pay off the balance as often as you wish, so long as you obey the credit card's terms. These terms usually involve paying your payments on time every month and not going over your credit line limit with your purchases. As you are allowed to keep borrowing against this credit limit indefinitely, creditors commonly call these credit cards open ended accounts or revolving accounts.

The Business Point of View

There is much that happens with credit cards beyond your consumer perspective. This behind the scenes activity explains why they offer you credit cards in the first place. When you give your credit card to the merchants to pay for your purchase, the credit card terminal of the merchant communicates with your card issuer electronically.

It asks the creditor if your card is valid for you to use and whether or not you have sufficient available credit. Your issuer of the credit card instantly reviews the charge before sending a reply back that this transaction either has been approved or alternatively declined.

Why does the credit card issuer provide you with this convenience? They receive several percent (typically from one to three percent) of the charged amount from the merchant in fees.

They also hope to make money off of your charges from you!

The creditor is providing you with a pre-set time limit to repay the entire amount that you have borrowed from them (usually a little less than a month). If you do not do this by the cut off date (the payment due date), then they will charge you interest. This amount of time before they assess interest charges is known as the grace period, and it typically lasts from 20 to 25 days.

Should you choose not to pay down your entire balance by the time this grace period ends, then they assess a finance charge and add this on to your remaining balance.

Your finance charge will be based upon the interest rate on your particular credit card multiplied by your outstanding balance.

This interest rate amounts to the yearly rate that you pay to borrow money using your credit card. The creditors typically base these interest rates on the prevailing market interest rate, the kind of credit card that you possess, and your credit history.

For those of you who have a good credit history of repaying credit card bills, you will secure a lower interest rate than the usually charged amount. Similarly if your credit history is less ideal, then you will generally pay a higher interest rate than the typical interest rate amount.

Businesses give you the chance to pay off your entire balance before this grace period ends so that you can avoid paying any interest. In reality, they would prefer that you did not repay it all at one time.

You must at least make the minimum payment amount by the time the due date arrives or you will receive a late fee. From your perspective, paying the minimum amount only every month is not only the slowest way to pay off your credit card bill, it is also the most costly way to pay this credit card balance down.

You should always pay at the very least the minimum amount due every month in order to have an on-time paying credit history. This will also save you late fees.

Ideally you should pay off all or most of your balance every month. With enough months paying your credit cards down on time, you can qualify for a better interest rate on your credit card.

How Long Does it Take to Build Good Credit?

You want to have instantly good credit, but it does not work that way. It would also defeat the purpose of the whole credit score idea if it did. More on that later. You will need about six months of on time payment history to have a decent credit score. The reason is that the most heavily used credit scoring system FICO requires at least six months of timely payments to produce a score.

VantageScore will do it in only a month or two, but since most credit checks involve FICO, this is less important. One of the main components of a credit score involves how long a credit history you have, which means that your score will improve over time with on time payments.

Another way to build credit history faster is to take advantage of parents with good credit. Your parents can add you as an authorized user. As an authorized user you will benefit immediately from the length of their credit history, which increases your score. This could also diversify the type of credit that appears on your report, similarly boosting your credit score.

Keeping accounts open that you do not use will also help to boost your score. You should avoid running cards too close to the limit as there are penalties for doing this. Instead try staying under 30 percent of your available limit to get the maximum points for this category.

Obtaining your first credit card or two is exciting. It does not automatically give you an over 800 point score. You need to make building good credit both a short and long term goal.

Know that good credit history stays on your report forever.

What Do I Need to Get a Credit Card?

What does it take to get your first credit card? You need an income in order to qualify for a credit card. The Credit Card Act of 2009 set new standards for protecting consumers. The act does not require a minimum income to get a credit card, but it does restrict issuing one to a person who can not make the minimum payments under credit card account terms.

You must be able to demonstrate an income that shows you have the capability to pay back the debt. The card issuers will consider a few factors besides income. They use these to determine your debt to income ratio, which compares your total monthly debt repayments to your available monthly income.

The ratio which the Consumer Financial Protection Bureau suggests is no higher than 43 percent. A credit card issuer will evaluate your debt to income figure to decide if you should have their credit card and how much of a limit you deserve.

They will also consider your credit history and credit score. Even if you do not have a credit card yet, you will have a credit history that is based on repayments of other debts such as student loans or car loans.

You do not need to file proof of income. If you apply online for a credit card, the application process includes a question on how much your income is.

Is It Ever Too Late to Build Credit?

No, it's never too late to work on building your credit. You may feel that in the second half of your life you have missed the credit train, but this is not the case.

Credit applications do not have any limitations or cutoffs.

The Equal Credit Opportunity Act prohibits creditors from discriminating against you due to your age. Credit does generally build up over time (or with age) if you are making good credit decisions, but it certainly does not take a lifetime for you to attain a good credit score.

The process for you to build credit is the same whether you have no credit or bad credit. It can be easiest to start with a secured credit card. This is a card that you make a security deposit on to obtain a credit line.

As you make the payments on time and all the time, your credit history will build and your score will increase.

It is always a good idea to make sure that your debt balance to credit limit ratio stays low. Your goal for this figure should be no higher than 30 percent.

Here is the breakdown of factors that determine your credit score:

- Payment history 35 percent
- Credit usage 30 percent
- Time of credit history 15 percent
- New credit 10 percent
- Types of credit you have 10 percent

Remember to check out your credit reports at least once each year for any mistakes. You need to dispute these if there are any errors.

Patience is your best ally in building up a strong credit history and score, so the earlier you start, the sooner you will reach your goals as with most things in life.

Is There a Minimum Age to Apply for a Credit Card?

You can not apply for a credit card by yourself until you are at least 18 years of age. This does not mean that you will automatically be approved for such a card when you become an adult.

Legally you are allowed to apply for your own credit card at 18, but the law on the subject mandates that you possess a steady income source in order to qualify. Your parents' monthly allowance will not be counted as income. Only with a reliable monthly income will you be able to repay charges that you make on your credit card so that you do not fall into a credit card debt trap.

When you are ready to apply for a first card, you should be on the lookout for those credit cards that target students. You might also apply for a retail credit card. Both types have a higher chance of approving you when you are just getting started as financially independent.

Another good choice is to obtain a secured credit card. By making a deposit, you gain a credit limit against this security. Two of these that are great for first time credit card holders are:

1. Capital One Secured Master Card
2. Discover It Secured

Both are tailored for you when you start to build up credit on your own.

How Many Credit Cards Should I Have?

You may want to know the perfect number of credit cards that you should have, but there is no ideal number. FICO has done a recent analysis of individuals with excellent credit scores over 800 (with 750 to 850 being considered the excellent category).

They found that these people have three open credit cards on average.

You should not be quick to close an account as this will reduce the total amount of credit that you have and could increase your debt to limit ratio at the same time. Both of these factors negatively affect your credit score. Open, inactive accounts do not hurt your score, but they can help it to be higher as they increase the total available credit that you have.

Opening a new credit card is a method for increasing your available credit.

Doing so permits you to charge more while still keeping a safe ratio of credit utilization. The lower your balance ratio is to your total available credit limit, the better off your score will be.

You should seek to maintain a utilization ratio that is under 30 percent. It is easy for you to figure out this ratio by totalling up your balances on all credit cards that you have and then dividing this by the total limits of all your cards. As an example, if you have a balance of $250 on a credit limit that totals $1,000, then your utilization ratio would be 25 percent.

I Don't Use My Credit Card, Should I Close It?

It may seem like common sense to close a credit card if you are not using it, but this is not usually the case. You should never be in a hurry to close out an existing credit account. The first reason is that closed accounts will be dropped from your credit report in time.

This would lower the average age component of your credit accounts.

Besides this, when you close one of your credit cards, you remove a portion of your total available credit. This action alone can create an immediate negative effect on your personal credit score.

Remember that open accounts which are inactive do not hurt your credit score, but they can boost it by raising your total available credit.

A reason that you might want to close a card that you are not using is if it comes with a yearly fee. Closing such a card would save you money. Before you do this, it is a smart idea to call the issuer of this credit card and ask them to either waive the annual fee (for a year or more) or to convert the card to another type of account that does not come with a yearly fee.

Doing so would enable you to keep the average account age higher for your credit report, which translates to higher credit scores in the end.

Remember that there is no harm in having an open credit card that sits idly in your wallet. Even unused it is creating benefits for your credit history and score.

Think carefully before closing any credit card account!

What is the Best Way to Pay Off My Student Loan?

If you are looking for the best way to pay off your student loan, there are several useful strategies that you can follow. The most effective method to pay down the loan quickly is to make a larger payment than the minimum amount that you owe every month.

It works because the more money you pay on your loan upfront, the lower amount of interest you will end up owing - and the faster your balance will go down.

Another way that you can make more payments without feeling the loss of the money is to do half of your payment amount every other week instead of waiting to make a full payment once per month. This will allow you to get in an additional full payment every year.

By reducing your interest costs, it will also help you to reduce your schedule for repayment.

If the interest rate on your student loan is higher, you can pay it down quicker by refinancing your student loans. This does not require you to put out more money in additional payments but it can significantly reduce the pay off time. Reducing your student loan interest rate from eight percent down to four percent would help you to pay off your balance around two years faster.

If your credit score is in the high 600 level, then you have a strong chance of being able to refinance for a better interest rate. The lender will also be interested in your income level and history of timely payments on bills.

The worst thing that you can do in paying off your student loans is to be consistently late with or even to miss payments. This will cause late payment penalties and missed payment fees to be added to your total balance.

What Do I Do Once I Get My First Credit Card?

There are few things as exciting for you as receiving approval on your first credit card. You will receive this card in the mail after the issuer sends it out to your credit card application listed address. The first thing to do after receiving your first credit card is to activate it.

You can not use it until you complete the activation process.

The front of your new card will contain a sticker that lists an Internet address and phone number to activate the card. In order to complete your activation, you will need to provide your social security number and/or your zip code along with your credit card number. Once you have activated the card, it is ready for you to use.

Do not give in to the temptation to rush immediately out and charge it though.

Although it may not be fun, you should read the credit card agreement that comes inside the envelope alongside your credit card. This is a detailed and long document complete with all terms and conditions attached to the credit card.

Important details that you will want to take note of include your new account's features, the charges that will apply to your card, penalties you will be assessed for being late with payments, and the proper way to address any disputes between you and the card issuer.

Reading over your agreement will enable you to better understand all of the responsibilities (it is likely you already know the benefits) that come with having this credit card.

You will want to understand your new card's assigned credit limit. This is the maximum dollar amount up to which you can charge your card. Your card will be declined if you exceed this amount unless you opt for over the limit charges.

Realize that charging your card up to the credit limit is not a responsible use of this new credit account. Doing so will hurt your credit score significantly.

Can I Check My Credit Score for Free?

It is easy for you to confuse checking your credit report and your credit score. You can check your credit score by signing up for a service that partners with one or more of the three main credit reporting agencies Experian, Equifax, or TransUnion.

Credit Karma is a leading example of such a free service, with over a hundred million members. Other services may entail either a charge or some other membership obligation, though they may allow you a free trial that you can cancel after checking your credit scores.

Many such services will also give you a different credit score than an inquiring lender will see. Please check the resource section at the end of the book where you'll find additional services besides CreditKarma.

Credit Karma provides the actual scores from the three credit reporting agencies!

You can easily check your credit reports for free. Every year, you are allowed to receive three free credit reports (one report from each of the reporting agencies). In cases where you think you might have become a victim of identity theft or fraud, you can obtain more free credit reports.

If a company rejects you for a credit decision, then you can also get another free credit report from the reporting agency that the lender used in making their decision.

In order to get your annual free credit reports from all three of the primary credit reporting agencies (Equifax, Experian, and TransUnion), you should either call 1-877-322-8228 or go to <u>AnnualCreditReport.com</u>.

After answering several questions and proving your identity, you will receive the reports either on your computer or smart device (if you applied online) or in the mail (if you called to request them).

You should not pay for your credit reports, neither to check your credit score!

Do I Have to Go Into Debt to Build Credit?

You may have heard a rumor that you have to take on debt in order to build up credit. This is among the most common myths surrounding credit cards today. It is simply not true that you must continuously carry credit card balances and have debt in order to improve your credit score. In fact the opposite can be the case.

Keeping a credit card balance that is excessively high will harm your personal credit score.

The best way to appropriately take advantage of your credit card to build up good credit is to charge items with the credit card, pay the entire balance every month (even better twice per months), and so build up a solid credit score without needing to get into debt. The key to doing this is for you to exercise discipline in not running up a balance that you can not pay down when the bill comes.

If you do carry a balance, work towards keeping the total debt to less than 30 percent of your available total credit. Any amount over this ratio will harm your credit score under the component of credit card usage, which accounts for 30 percent of your possible credit score.

Exceeding 30 percent (and especially going over 50 percent) will significantly reduce the amount of points you receive in this important credit scoring category.

Which is More Important:
Payment History or Credit Utilization?

You will want to be aware of which credit profile component is most important for your credit score. The different components of credit score are:

- Your payment history for 35 percent
- Your credit utilization for 30 percent
- The length of your credit history for 15 percent
- The different mix of credit you possess for 10 percent
- New credit you have obtained for 10 percent

The breakdown means that payment history is slightly more important than credit utilization. Since they are only five percentage points apart though, they are very close in importance to one another.

Will Checking My Credit Report Hurt My Credit Scores?

You might be concerned that getting a copy of your credit report could hurt your credit scores. The good news is that pulling your own report is not considered to be an inquiry on new credit. It does not have any effect on your score. It is a smart idea to routinely review your own credit report as a matter of fact.

Performing a self check on your report will allow you to make certain that the information which the credit reporting bureaus are sharing with lending companies is both current and accurate.

Each of the three main credit reporting bureaus (Experian, TransUnion, and Equifax) will provide you with a free copy of your credit report once per year. If you are denied credit or you feel your identity has been stolen, you can request additional copies of your report at no cost.

You might also want to keep a close eye on your credit score. You can do this by signing up for free with Credit Karma. There is a common myth that checking your own score will harm it, but this is not the case. When you check your own credit score, it does not impact the result. However, if credit card companies or lenders check your score, this could lower it.

When either you or a lender checks your score, it will show up on your personal credit report as an inquiry. When you use a third party service like Credit-Karma, you can check your score as often as you like without creating any inquiries.

This means that when you apply for credit, you will see the credit card issuers or lending companies listed on your credit report under inquiries.

The credit report will also contain records for any lenders to which you did not apply who pulled your credit.

What is a Good Credit Score?

With all of the importance attached to credit scores, you want to know what a good score actually is. Credit scores range from 300 to 850 for both FICO and Vantage scoring models. The general breakdown is that 700 or higher is considered to be good. Meanwhile a score of 800 and up is called excellent.

Under a percent of American consumers have perfect credit (of 850).

Getting even an excellent score is more possible than you might believe. Major credit bureau Experian provides a breakdown of the score categories along with the percentages of consumers who fall into each category. According to Experian, 19.9 percent of consumers have an excellent score of 800-850.

The credit bureau states that 18.2 percent of people possess a very good score of from 740 to 799. Another 21.5 percent have what they call a good score of 670 to 739. Consumers with a fair credit score of from 580 to 669 equate to 20.2 percent. A last 17 percent of Americans have a poor credit score of from 300 to 579.

Of the whole adult American population, 19 percent (around 45 million adults) do not have a credit score at all. They are called credit invisible by the Consumer Financial Protection Bureau. The reasons for this are that they lack any meaningful history of using credit, or the information on how they have used it is limited. It explains why they do not have a credit score.

Building up a good credit score is easier than you might think. The two most important categories that the credit bureaus consider are payment history (for 35 percent of the breakdown) and credit utilization (for 30 percent).

By paying your bills on time every month and not using more than 30 percent of your total available credit, you will be on your way to possessing a good credit score.

Do Joint Credit Cards Help Build Good Credit?

If you are trying to build up good credit, getting a joint credit card with a family member (who has good credit) could be the answer to doing so more quickly. The reason is that if two people share a joint credit card account, then the card's history becomes included on the two sets of credit reports. If your parents or spouse have better credit then you, they can share the benefit of having been approved for credit cards by themselves.

Doing so will also allow you to get a better interest rate than you could on your own without good credit. For many people with little or poor credit, being made a joint user is the only sure way to get a good credit card with that coveted lower interest rate.

This arrangement only works if the credit card is properly managed, with you keeping a low balance and making timely payments.

Both, you and the joint account holder share legal responsibility for the monthly payments. If you fall behind on the payments, the issuer can pursue both of you to recover payment. You could both suffer from legal action or lawsuits and have wage garnishments should the payments become seriously delinquent.

If you are both responsible, then the joint credit card strategy is a good idea for building up good credit.

Should I Consolidate My Credit Card Debt?

If you have a number of balances on credit cards, then you might be considering consolidating your credit card debt. Consolidating debt gathers your higher interest rate debts (such as credit cards) and rolls them over into one lower interest rate payment.

By reducing the total interest you pay, it reduces your total debt and helps you to pay it down quicker.

There are three main ways for you to consolidate your debt. The first is to take a low interest (or zero percent interest) credit card balance transfer offer. If a credit card offers you this arrangement, it will allow you to receive this lower interest rate until the end of the promotional period.

You should make it a goal to pay down the balance within that time frame. The interest rates typically default to a much higher amount after the promotional period ends.

The second way is to obtain a fixed interest rate debt consolidation loan. You use the loan money to pay off the credit card debt. The instalment loan allows you to pay this back in monthly payments over a pre-determined term.

Finally, you could also take a home equity loan and use the money to consolidate your credit card bills. There is a risk involved in this if you do not make the loan payments; you could lose your house to foreclosure. In all cases, your options will be limited by your credit profile and score and debt to income ratio.

Good to excellent credits scores range from about 700 to 850 and will give you more options to consolidate your credit card debt into a single payment.

Consolidating your debt is a strategy that you can easily pursue without having to seek a credit repair firm or lawyer's help.

What is a Good Credit Score to Buy a House?

If you are preparing to buy a house, you will need to know what a good credit score is to be approved for a home loan. The majority of conventional mortgages demand a 620 or higher FICO credit score to approve you. If your loan is backed up by the FHA Federal Housing Administration, then the required score drops to minimally 500 with a 10 percent down payment and to at least 580 with a 3.5 percent down payment.

Credit Karma has done a survey of over a million of its members who purchased a home with a first time mortgage between August of 2017 and 2018 to come up with average Vantage 3.0 credit score numbers for homebuyers.

This survey revealed that the Vantage Score for first time American home buyers is 684.

The figure varied widely by the state and city in which you live. The Vantage Score range of credit scores for first time home buyers was from 662 to 730 (again depending on the state in which you live). Buyers in states in the Northeast and West Coast (Washington, California, and Hawaii) showed the highest credit scores while those who live in the Gulf Coast and Appalachian states of the South had the lowest credit scores.

The credit score you need to buy a house also depends on the price of the home involved. In states where the average homes are more expensive like Hawaii (at an average of around $528,000 for a first time mortgage), the average credit score of home buyers was 715.

In states like Indiana where the average first time home loan is $196,000, the home buyer's score averages at 670. So while you might get an FHA loan in the 500 to 580 credit score range and a traditional mortgage for at least a 620 score, first time homebuyers' credit scores are often significantly higher, in the 662 to 730 range.

Do I Need to Have a Credit Card to Improve My Score?

If you do not have a credit card you may wonder is it important for your credit score that you get one. The fact is, that employing a credit card in your financial life directly impacts the most critical factors that make up your personal credit score. This includes a timely payment history (35 percent of the total) and credit card utilization (30 percent).

Obtaining a credit card to use routinely (but responsibly) is among the fastest and most efficient means of either building up or rebuilding your credit profile and score.

Keep in mind that credit scores quantify the way that you manage money which you borrow and repay. Having good credit requires that you possess a solid record of timely debt payments. Not making payments on something like a credit card means that you not only do not have good credit, but you also may have no credit. Making regular charges on a credit card allows you to build up credit without having to go into debt.

So long as you completely pay off your credit card balance every month on time, your issuer will report these credit card payments to each of the three main credit bureaus.

Treating your credit card like it is a debit card (charging only things that you can pay for each month) will keep you from paying interest on purchases and allow you to rapidly build up your credit.

Just remember that you need to keep your charges each month to less than 30 percent of your credit card total available balances so that you do not lose points in the critical credit card utilization category (the second most important consideration for FICO credit scores).

How Does Divorce Affect My Credit Report?

With so many people divorced these days, it is important to know how this will impact your credit report. The good news is that divorce does not directly affect your credit scores. Instead the financial issues that swirl around the proceedings can cause you to miss payments or to be late with them, lowering your score and hurting your credit history.

A common problem from messy divorces is that the attorney fees can wipe you out financially. If you are unable to keep up with your bills, this will impact the 35 percent FICO credit score category of timely payment history. If you no longer have enough income to keep up with your expenses after the divorce, you also may turn to using your credit cards to fill the gap. This would cause your credit card balance utilization (the second most important category at 30 percent) to become dangerously high (over the 30 percent FICO looks at) in short order.

Another problem could surround who will pay the bills on joint accounts like mortgages and credit cards. The divorce court judge may rule that your spouse is required to make the payments. If your spouse has a lower credit score and is unconcerned with this, they simply may not make the payments.

A spouse might also be resentful of making payments for assets that were awarded to you (like a home). Because your name is also on the joint accounts, late payments and delinquent accounts will adversely affect your credit score and history too.

The credit bureaus do not know or care if you are married or divorced. This status does not even show up in any of your credit history. They do notate all names on the accounts regarding repayment issues though.

Where Can I Get My Free Credit Reports?

The government enforces a law that requires the three major credit bureaus to send you a full credit report by request every year. Without having to sign up for anything, you can request one free credit report from Experian, Equifax, and TransUnion every 12 months.

If you are rejected from a credit application or job offer, or have your identity stolen, you can obtain additional free credit reports from the three main bureaus as well.

These free and full reports are easiest to obtain online by going to www.annualcreditreport.com.

This site is the only government authorized website from which you can directly download your full length, free credit reports.

You can also get these through the mail by calling 1-877-322-8228. In either case, you will be required to prove your identity by confirming your name, social security number, address, and date of birth.

You can also get free credit reports (that are not completely full versions) from credit monitoring services such as Credit Karma and Discover Credit Scoreboard. Credit Karma provides TransUnion credit reports while Discover Credit gives you Experian reports. Neither site requires you to make any financial or trial basis commitments or to link a credit card in order to use their legitimately free services.

You can obtain these reports as often as you like with either service.

What is Credit Counselling?

If you feel like you need additional help in managing your finances and debt, credit counselling is a good choice for you. Credit counselling is actually a phone call with a licensed credit counsellor that takes anywhere from 20 minutes to an hour.

This is a free resource which not for profit financial educational organizations offer you and other consumers.

In the call, the counsellor will go through your consumer debt, credit reports, and budget with you. Their goal is to help you better your financial situation by offering you advice and feedback on improving your own unique situation. This could include providing you with resources and tools to assist you in regaining control over your finances.

They can do this through offering more specialized counselling such as credit and debt counselling, mortgage counselling, student loan counselling, and other types of help.

One thing that credit counselling does not automatically include is a debt management plan. Debt management assists you in becoming free from debt quicker through reducing your interest rates and coming up with a repayment schedule.

A DMP would negatively impact your credit reports and score significantly.

This is why such a solution should only be offered as a matter of last resort. You should be wary of any credit counsellors who suggest that a debt management plan is your best and only choice.

What is the Difference Between a Charge Card and a Credit Card?

The primary difference is that typical charge cards do not provide credit. Instead they require you to pay off the entire balance each month.

With credit cards, you can pay down your purchases over months (or years). You will be charged interest for not paying the full balance by the payment due date. Charge cards have dwindled away until American Express remains the only significant charge card issuer within the United States.

Most retail stores have replaced their charge cards with revolving credit cards.

Charge cards look and work like credit cards when it comes to making purchases. They both have such common elements as travel perks and rewards. Yet charge cards do not offer balance transfers (with their attractive zero percent interest rate promotions) as they do not allow you to carry a balance.

Charge cards offer a few key benefits. They do not come with a pre-determined credit limit. This feature allows you to do large purchases on the card. Instead the amount that you can charge is determined by your credit score and history, payment history, financial resources, and typical charge card use. You can determine your charge card spending limit online or over the phone (the number is printed on the card's reverse). In contrast, credit cards always come with a pre-set limit that does not change often.

Another benefit to charge cards is that they do not include interest or incur debt. This is because you will be required to pay the balance in full each month. The charge card forces discipline on your finances this way. The principle has been diluted by American Express sometimes offering a "Pay Over Time" feature. This separate account within the card only applies to larger purchases (in excess of $100) as well as travel purchases that are eligible.

The "Pay Over Time" feature comes with finance charges if you do not pay the balance in full when it is due.

A key benefit from charge cards has always been their generous perks and rewards, particularly where travel is concerned. This is less of an absolute advantage these days as some credit cards (like the Chase Sapphire Preferred Card) now offer many features and rewards that are comparable to American Express' rewards program.

A last key benefit is the impact on credit scores of using charge cards. Scoring models (like FICO and Vantage Score) do not take charge card balances into account with their credit utilization component.

Since they can not calculate a ratio on these charge card balances without a limit, you can make larger or more purchases in a given month without negatively impacting your credit score.

Do I Have to Wait 7 Years to Get Good Credit After Problems in the Past?

Unfortunately, seven years is the time length for many kinds of negative items listed on your credit report to disappear. Late payments, charged off accounts, debt collection efforts, and Chapter 13 bankruptcy are all included in the seven years to drop off your report. Other more serious items like tax liens you have not paid, judgments, and Chapter 7 bankruptcy can stay on your report for longer than seven years.

The reason that seven years is significant is that the majority of negative reported items drop off your credit report at this point. This will not cancel the debts (if they are unpaid especially). You will still owe the debt even if it has been dropped from your credit report.

These debt collectors, lenders, and creditors may still pursue various legal means to collect these debts that are no longer listed. They can send letters, call you, or garnish wages with court permission.

Some states allow creditors to sue to collect a debt for longer than seven years, according to the state's statute of limitations.

You can engage a credit repair firm or debt lawyer to help challenge negative items on your personal credit report. If they are successful in getting these items overturned, then the negative items on your report will be dropped when the matter is resolved instead of over seven years.

How Much Will Bankruptcy Hurt My Credit Report?

Chapter 7 bankruptcy will impact your credit report for a full seven years. Its effects vary based on how high your credit score is when you file.

FICO released case specific information back in 2010 on how bankruptcy will impact your personal credit score. In two scenarios, they revealed that a person with a 780 credit score could lose as much as 240 points while another with a 680 credit score could lose up to 150 points.

The person with the higher score suffers a greater point loss. Both cases have your credit score settling at approximately the same level of 540 and 530. Should credit issues have already dragged your score down into the 500's, then your score has already been negatively impacted to a large degree and you have less to lose.

These are only examples. Your score could suffer less or even a little more depending on your personal credit and debt circumstances when you file for bankruptcy.

FICO does not distinguish between Chapter 13 and Chapter 7 bankruptcies which cover personal debt discharge.

It is worth noting that Chapter 7 ends fastest in only a matter of months following filing if you qualify. Chapter 13 bankruptcies take years to exit from as they involve from three to five years plans of repayment.

Will Bankruptcy Clear All of My Debts?

The reason you may seek to file bankruptcy is to clear away your debts that you can not pay. Whether or not this will happen depends on the type of bankruptcy for which you are approved. A discharge does release you from all personal liability of the debt. It also stops the creditor from continuing to pursue collection activity against you. Under such a discharge you are not required legally to repay these debts.

Some debts can not be discharged completely. Liens that are not addressed during the bankruptcy case stay in force. Secured creditors are able to enforce these liens so that they can reclaim the secured property.

A car payment is a good example. If you do not commit to a reaffirmation agreement on your car payment, the debt discharge would erase your obligation to pay back the loan. You would not be able to keep the car in such a scenario as the lender would have lien rights to repossess it.

In the vast majority of cases, if you file a Chapter 7 bankruptcy and it is approved by the judge, then you will obtain a debt discharge at the conclusion of the case.

The Chapter 7 process generally gives this discharge 60 days following the Meeting of Creditors (according to 341(a) statute requirements). This usually means that you would get your discharge around four months after you file your original petition for a Chapter 7 bankruptcy.

It is important to know that Chapter 13 bankruptcy will not clear all of your debt. Instead it would make repayment arrangements that stretch from three to five years long.

What is Credit Repair?

Credit repair refers to fixing bad credit that could have declined for a number of differing reasons. This could be as easy as filing disputes for mistaken information with the main credit bureaus Experian, Equifax, and Trans-Union. It could be more involved if there has been identity theft and resulting damage to your credit report. In this case, more significant work is required to clear up credit A third type of credit repair involves addressing key financial issues and lenders' concerns.

It requires both effort and time to correct inaccurate information on credit reports. Third parties are not able to remove information held by the credit reporting bureaus. Instead this information (if it is inaccurate or falsely represented) may be disputed. This can be done by you personally or a credit repair company on your behalf.

You or a credit repair company can file disputes when you find missing, inaccurate, or incomplete information on your credit reports. Catching this information and getting it corrected is critical in repairing your credit. Other ways that you can repair your credit focus on addressing your own credit activity and credit utilization.

Just getting your credit card balances down to 30 percent or less of your total available credit will add significant points to your credit score. The credit utilization is the second most important factor of your credit score (at a 30 percent component).

You can also repair your credit by making timely payments, which improves the most important component (that makes up 35 percent of your score).

What is Credit Monitoring?

Credit monitoring services are commercial endeavors that charge a fee to watch over your credit reports. They alert you if they discover any changes to your accounts (or new accounts) detailed in your credit report. If another individual attempts to use your data to open a new credit account, the service will tell you immediately (so that you do not wait to discover the damage for months of even years). They can send out these alert messages via text message, email, or phone calls.

Credit monitoring services charge prices ranging from $9.99 to $29.99 per month. It is important for you to understand what you are receiving before you commit to these fees.

Be especially wary about offers for free credit monitoring.

Because of several major data breaches that occurred in recent years, you may be eligible to receive free credit monitoring. Equifax suffered a massive breach in 2017, and Capital One did as well in 2019. Equifax provides four years of free credit monitoring (from all three major credit reporting bureaus) to anyone who was impacted by this.

You can take advantage of it by signing up before January 22, 2020. Capital One notified all Americans whose Social Security numbers were stolen. If you were affected, they provide you with two years of free credit monitoring services (as well as identity protection) via TransUnion.

If you were not awarded free credit monitoring by the data breaches, you can always buy the service on your own. Make certain you understand all services that are included, your rights (and windows) for cancellation, and what rights you have should the service fail to protect you.

You can also take the most important step to protect yourself without paying for credit monitoring. Anyone may obtain a credit freeze by calling the credit reporting bureaus.

Analysts call such a freeze the strongest type of protection from identity theft that will keep them from accessing your credit (without having specific permission).

What is Debt Consolidation?

Debt consolidation is the rolling over of high interest debt (like credit card bills) to a lower interest payment loan with a single payment. Pursuing debt consolidation can help you to lower the total amount of debt you have to repay and to better organize it to pay it down quicker.

Two main types of debt consolidation help you to reorganize your debt. You could apply for a debt consolidation loan at a fixed interest rate. When you get this money, you then apply it to pay your other debts off. You pay the debt consolidation loan for a set term in monthly instalments.

The other primary method is with a zero percent or low interest balance transfer offer from a credit card. These offers permit you to transfer your other credit card bills onto the card and then pay off your balance (preferably within the promotional period).

If you own a house, you might also consider taking a home equity loan for debt consolidation purposes. The risk of this is that it puts your home in danger if you are unable to repay the loan. Your best option with debt consolidation comes down to your credit history and score, alongside your personal debt to income ratio.

In order to be successful with debt consolidation, you need several things. Your aggregate debt (not counting mortgage debt) should not be higher than 40 percent of your gross income. You also need sufficiently good credit to be approved for a debt consolidation loan at a low interest rate or for a zero percent credit card balance transfer offer. It is essential that you have enough cash flow to continuously service your debt.

Finally, you should make a plan to not incur a large amount of debt for the future.

What is Debt Settlement?

Debt settlement is a third party company service that attempts to decrease the debt you owe by arranging for discounted settlements with creditors and debt collectors. Debt settlement firms can reduce the debt you owe, but this is usually done at the expense of harming your credit. These programs and their services charge fees that could increase your debt.

Other names for debt settlement firms are debt adjusting and debt relief companies. They operate by talking with your creditors for you to negotiate a lower payment and interest rate. Sometimes they can reduce the total debt you owe or settle your debt for a lump sum amount.

For these services, they charge a percentage of the total of savings they arrange for you in the debt restructuring.

Firms which attempt to settle all debts for single lump sum payments will often require you to make routine deposits into an account you control while they negotiate on your behalf. A third party administers this account and the money you save to pay out lump sum settlement payments on your debt.

Your debt consolidation company may suggest that you stop paying your bills until they reach the settlement arrangement. This can negatively impact your credit as well.

After the debt settlement firm has reached agreement with your creditors and reduced minimally one of your debts, you will have to consent to their terms to make at least one payment to the debt collector or creditor for this settled amount. At this point, the debt settlement firm is able to assess you fees for the services they performed on your behalf.

How do I Dispute My Credit Report Online?

Disputing information on your credit report *online* is the fastest way to accomplish this task. If you find something that is incorrect or incomplete while reviewing your credit reports, you can file directly with the credit reporting bureau that has the inaccurate information.

Doing so requires that you go to:
www.TransUnion.com
www.Experian.com
www.Equifax.com

It takes only minutes of your time and it is completely free to dispute any false items on your reports. You could also call the bureaus or write them to dispute incorrect information, but this would be considerably slower.

Equifax gives the steps to filing a dispute online. You start by checking your credit report to find any incomplete or inaccurate information. Should you see any information that needs to be corrected, you then click the options on the applicable credit reporting bureau to file a dispute.

The three credit bureaus claim that they will start investigating the matter immediately. Despite this urgency, it can take them up to 30 days to complete the investigation and to get back with you. The good news is that if the bureau(s) find any information that should be corrected or updated, they will take care of the updates for you.

Equifax also suggests if you find information from a creditor or lender that is false or incomplete then you contact the lender or creditor who issued your account directly. Doing so may speed up the process of getting the information corrected when the credit bureau contacts the creditor or lender to verify the information.

The bureaus will attempt to update any information on your report from the data you supply them. If it involves material that has been submitted by a third party lender or creditor though, the credit bureau will have to investigate it with them directly.

How Long Does Negative Information Stay on My Credit Report?

The amount of time negative information stays on your credit report depends on which type of debt it is. Thanks to the federal law the Fair Credit Reporting Act, there is a specific time limit allowed by law. For most types of negative information, a seven year credit reporting limit exists from the date of original delinquency. This includes late payments and collections on credit cards, student loan defaults, and foreclosures. The Higher Education Act specifically deals with student loan defaults.

Certain items may stay on your report for longer than seven years. Charge offs can remain on your report for seven and a half years from the date the creditor charges them off.

Generally they only report for seven years as with delinquent payments.

Judgments and lawsuits vary from seven years from the filing date up to the statute of limitations from the state (whichever is longer). Paid tax liens require seven years from the date you pay them (or to the point you ask the IRS to remove them if they do not do it automatically).

Unpaid tax liens remain on your credit report indefinitely. Bankruptcies require typically seven years from the date of filing though they can stay as long as 10 years from the original filing date. Regardless of the type of bad credit information, you can expect at least seven years of negative impact on your credit report (from the point your creditors start reporting it as negative).

How Do I Get Credit When No One Wants to Give it to Me?

It is not easy to get credit for the first time. The catch 22 is that you can not get credit because you do not have any yet. The majority of creditors want you to have credit before they will extend you any.

The best way around this is to seek out a credit card whose target audience is people who do not yet have credit. For those of you with a savings or checking account, you can ask your bank about a credit offer for customers with limited credit histories. Many banks offer customers student credit cards, credit builder loans, or secured credit cards.

To get a student credit card in your own name, you must be at least 18 years old.

Applying for a secured credit card is another easier way to get started with first time credit. These cards typically require that you make a deposit against the credit limit on your new card. In this way, it works almost like a debit card.

The good thing about some of these secured card offers is that they will automatically convert to non secured credit cards after you have a proven timely payment history of from 12 to 18 months with them.

Another option is to apply for a gas credit card or retail store card. These are usually easier to qualify for as a first time credit applicant. After you build up several months of positive credit history with either of these types, it will be simpler to be qualified for one of the major branded credit cards such as Mastercard or Visa.

The downside to gas and retail cards is that they come with higher costs. The interest rates will be higher on both types than they are with typical Visa or Mastercards. This is the trade off for building up credit with these gas and retail cards. So long as you pay off all of your balance every month, you will not incur any finance charges. This discipline will serve you well when you get your major brand credit cards.

Can I Build Credit by Paying My Rent on Time?

If you do not have much of a credit history, you can expand it by paying your rent on time, according to credit reporting bureau Experian. The bureau considers rental payment information that is reported to their Experian RentBureau in their credit reports. This means that timely rent payments will be incorporated into your standard personal credit report. Some credit scores will take this rent payment history into account.

Such positive rent payment history helps you to rebuild or establish first time credit history.

The way it works is through either the property management company or the electronic rent payment service providing the information to Experian Rent Bureau. They update this information once every 24 hours. It is important information for companies that do resident screening when you apply to be an apartment resident.

Communication companies, auto finance firms, and banks will also consider this item on your credit reports when they are evaluating credit worthiness.

You may need to ensure that your rent payments are being reported to the major credit bureaus. If you are about to rent or are already renting, ask the property management company if they report rental payment information to the bureaus. Should your property management company or landlord not report this data, you can enrol in a rental payment service that works with the bureaus (like Experian Rent Bureau).

Not only do these services report your history of rental payments to the credit reporting bureaus, but they also make it easy to pay your rent electronically through your bank. Some of the major companies that provide this service are Rent Track, Pay Lease, eRent Payment, Pay Your Rent, and Clear Now.

How to Build Credit With Help From Mom or Dad?

Two great ways that mom and/or dad can help you with your financial start is by making you an authorized user on a credit card they have or by co-signing a loan together. Other family members or close friends could also do this for you.

By making you an authorized user, your parents get you a credit card with your name on it. They can benefit by helping you this way if it is a rewards credit card. You will receive credit history credit for the timely payments they make on the card account. Your parents will earn either cash back or points for every dollar in purchases you make.

There are two things your parents will need to consider. There could be yearly fees for having authorized users. The other is that they are responsible for repaying any charges that you make even if you do not pay for them.

If your spending significantly increases their debt load (credit card utilization), then both of your credit scores will be harmed.

The second way your parents can help is by co-signing on a car loan, student loan, or for a credit card. If your parents have good credit, this will significantly improve your chances of successfully qualifying. With a co-signed loan, you are both responsible for repaying the credit or loan.

If you are under 21 years of age, the Credit Card Accountability Responsibility and Disclosure Act from 2009 (CARD) mandates that you must have a co-signer who is an adult, unless you can demonstrate enough independent income of your own to pay back credit card charges and balances.

How Do I Increase My Credit Limit?

It can be beneficial to increase your credit limit if you are financially stable. If you are able to pay your credit card bills on time and in full each month, then expanding your credit limit will improve your credit scores as it reduces your credit utilization ratio (the second most important FICO score component at 30 percent). A higher credit limit will also increase your financial flexibility. Increasing your limit can be a bad thing if you struggle with overspending tendencies.

There are four ways to grow your credit limit.

You can go to the credit card company website to make an online request. A great number of the issuers have this feature built into their website. After signing in, you should see a menu option to make an increase request. The creditor may ask you to provide updated information on your income. If you can show a higher income, this demonstrates better financial security. Many credit issuers will consider this as they review your credit line increase request.

Another way to request an increase is by calling the creditor. Their number is listed on the back of your credit card. Start by querying the customer service representative if you are eligible for a credit line increase. They will likely ask if your income has increased as well as why you want the higher limit.

You could also wait for automatic credit line increases. Many creditors provide these periodically after you have used the card responsibly for six months or a year.

Finally, you can always apply for a new credit card. You are more likely to receive this if you have been timely in your payments on your existing credit cards. The same creditor may be willing to offer you another card that possesses a higher limit in lieu of the original one. Otherwise, you may simply receive a second credit card. Either way, you will have a higher overall available credit limit than you did before.

How Do I Compare Credit Cards?

Nowadays online sites like Nerd Wallet and Wallet Hub provide you with free credit card offer comparisons screening tools. These permit you to line up the various credit cards that are most relevant to you so that you can compare them by interest rates, rewards, cash back, balance transfer offers, business features, bad credit, and more.

These handy online apps allow you to apply specific filters in their comparison tools. After you have checked the features that are most important to you, they will return a list of credit cards that match your specified profile.

Comparing credit cards like this before you apply for them will save too many hard hits on your credit reports that could damage your credit score.

Other sites like Credit Karma actually ask you a series of questions (four with Credit Karma) and then reveal the best cards in each category. They tell you to think about your credit (know your credit score and be realistic) and then determine if you will carry a balance or pay off the charges every month. You have to tell them if you want to transfer a balance.

Finally they ask if you are more interested in travel rewards or cash back programs. Credit Karma then reveals to you the best cards for your situation. At the time of publication, these categories were improving your credit (Capital One Secured Mastercard), paying lower interest rates (Chase Freedom Unlimited), earning cash back (Citi Double Cash Card), earning travel rewards (Chase Sapphire Preferred Card), and transferring a balance (Chase Slate).

How Long Do Late Payments Stay in My Credit Report?

Late credit card and loan payments can remain up to seven years on your credit report. What makes the answer a little less precise is that every lender is allowed to decide what they consider to be a late payment and the point when they report it as late to one of the credit bureaus (Experian, Equifax, and TransUnion).

For the majority of cases, when you are more than 30 days past due on your payment the lender or creditor will notify major credit bureaus. At this point, your late payment would appear on your personal credit reports.

A delinquency like this would usually drop off of the credit reports after seven years from the first date of delinquency.

Consider an example. If you experienced a 30 day late payment that the creditor reported in June of 2018 and you made the account current by July of 2018, then the late payment notification would fall of your credit reports in June of 2025. If you were late on two consecutive payments, the 60 day late payment notice from June of 2018 that you caught up on in August of 2018 would still disappear from your report in June of 2025.

Late payments will have their greatest effect on your credit score when they are first reported. The good news is that with the aging late payment notice, the effect on your credit score should be less. Each of the three credit bureaus maintains its own rules for evaluating your credit history information and so generating your credit score.

Late payments can cause a larger impact on one credit score than another because of this. It explains why there is variance between the credit scores generated by the different three major bureaus.

Does Opening a New Credit Card Hurt My Credit Score?

The answer to this question depends on four factors. If you are opening your first credit card, a new card account could improve your credit score. Without a credit card it is possible that you do not even possess a credit score. After six months of this new account, enough information will exist for the credit score calculation to create a score for you.

For other scenarios, opening a new card can hurt your score some. It creates a hard inquiry that shows up on your credit report when you apply. This remains whether or not you accept the card or receive approval for it. Since these types of inquiries are a 10 percent component of your credit score, every subsequent hard inquiry could mean the loss of several points on your credit score. This could be the difference between a good and bad credit score (translating to a good interest rate and a mediocre one on a loan).

Another factor with a new card is that new credit cards reduce the age of your average credit. Another 15 percent of your score component comes from the age of your credit (measuring your experience in managing credit). All else being equal the greater your credit experience, the higher your score will be. Two elements make up your credit age component. It measures the age of your original account as well as your average length of history for all accounts.

The longer it has been since you opened your last account, the more this will reduce the average age for your credit accounts.

The last factor has to do with credit utilization, which makes up 30 percent of your credit score. If you do not make major purchases on your new credit card, then your credit utilization ratio will drop and so improve your score. Should you open a new account and immediately run up the balance, then your credit utilization may increase enough to cause a substantial hit. You should seek to keep this credit utilization number below 30 percent (and even better under 10 percent) as much as possible.

The more of your new credit limit you are using, the worse the impact on your credit score will be.

Will My Credit Score Go Down if I am Denied a Credit Card?

According to credit bureau Experian, being denied a credit card will not cause your credit score to go down because you were rejected. The reason is that your credit report does not provide details on whether or not any application has been declined or approved. Since the credit bureaus do not know, a decline does not create an impact on a credit score.

Applying for the card does create a hard inquiry though. Such an inquiry demonstrates that you applied to obtain more debt even though the available credit or debt does not yet show up on your personal credit report. The fact that no new account appears on your report does not mean your application was denied. It alternatively could mean that you decided not to accept the credit account or loan.

Applying for a credit card (whether it is accepted or rejected) does harm your credit score in the 10 percent component for new credit inquiries. This results from the bureaus understanding that possible new debt creates potential credit risk. The good news is that such an effect is usually quite small. It will decline in importance with time too.

Remember that timely payment history on approved accounts (at a 35 percent of credit score component) is the most important element in your credit scoring.

To put this into perspective, this payment history outweighs the impact of new credit inquiries by three and one half times.

What is the Best Credit Card for Travel and Airline Miles?

The Chase Sapphire Preferred credit card has been named the best credit card for travel and airline miles by many top review sites including Forbes.com. One of its greatest appeals is the upfront sign up bonus. Once you spend $4,000 over the first three months, you receive 60,000 points.

These points translate to $750 in tangible travel using Chase's travel portal. You can exchange them for more than this amount even by transferring them to Chase's loyalty partners including Southwest, United, and Hyatt.

Besides this upfront bonus, the Sapphire Preferred card gives you double points for every dollar you spend on restaurants and travel anywhere in the world. When you book travel arrangements using Chase Ultimate Rewards, you get 25 percent additional value on hotels, airfare, cruises, and car rentals.

The card allows you to receive one for one point transfers to many frequent traveller programs. These include the British Airways Executive Club, Air France KLM Flying Blue, Korean Air Skypass, Virgin Atlantic Flying Club, United Mileage Plus, Southwest Airlines Rapid Rewards, Marriot Rewards, IHG Rewards Club, World of Hyatt, and Ritz Carlton Rewards.

The card includes no foreign transaction fees for purchases overseas. It does have a $95 annual fee of which you should be aware.

The Capital One Venture Rewards Credit Card is often listed as the runner up for best travel and airlines rewards miles. You are allowed to redeem your miles on any travel purchases, whether or not they are a travel partner.

Among its big appeals is a double miles earned per dollar bonus on all purchase in whatever category. By spending $3,000 in the first three months, you earn the sign up bonus of 50,000 miles.

What is the Best Credit Card to Start Building Credit?

The best of so-called starter credit cards were crafted with new cardholders like you in mind. Each of the best new credit accounts will report your timely payment history to each of the three major credit bureaus. While secured credit cards are a great option for new credit holders, there are some that do not require these deposits upfront.

The Discover It Student Cash Back card does not require a security deposit. This card intended for students just getting started with credit allows you to enrol every quarter to get five percent cash back from grocery stores, gas stations, restaurants, and Amazon.com among other places. Other purchases will earn you one percent limitless cash back.

The Capital One Platinum Credit Card promises you a starter credit line upfront with an increased limit once you have successfully paid your first five months' payments on time. It also provides no yearly fees, balance transfer fees, or foreign transaction fees.

Among the best secured starter credit cards is the Discover It Secured. This card mandates that you pay at least a $200 security deposit but will allow you to deposit upwards of $2,500 when you open the account to have a larger credit limit.

Discover refunds you this security deposit after you have proven your payment history by transitioning you to a traditional Discover credit card. The card gives two percent cash back on purchases you make per quarter at restaurants and gas stations to your fist thousand dollars in charges there, then it gives you one percent cash back afterwards and on all other kinds of purchases. Discover also matches all of your earned cash back at the conclusion of your first year with them.

If you have bad or little credit, Capital One Secured Mastercard offers a $200 credit line with security deposit ranging from $49 to $200. Once you make your on time first five payments, they will offer you an improved credit line. It comes with no yearly fees, car rental and accident insurance, free credit score access each month, and extended warranty coverage.

Is it Possible to Have Too Many Credit Cards?

There is no straightforward answer to the question how many credit cards are too many. The average American has three open credit cards. If you have so many that you can not manage to keep up with the monthly payments, due dates, interest rates, fees, charges, and other important information then this is too many.

Too many credit cards can cause you to have a higher debt to income ratio. Lenders contemplate your available credit and treat it as potential debt when they evaluate your loan applications. If they calculate assuming that all of your cards get maxed out, then this may cause your debt to income ratio to be treated as over 37 percent.

This is a point where you might consider closing credit card accounts (newest ones first to not impact your average credit length history too much).

With more credit cards, you may be tempted to use them to excess. It is important to keep your total credit utilization to less than 30 percent and ideally under 10 percent (this component comprises 30 percent of your credit score). The simple way to minimize your credit utilization is to keep a smaller number of cards.

You might be better served to have other types of credit in lieu of more credit cards. Credit score algorithms consider the kinds of credit you have to ascertain how much experience you have with other types of credit. Credit mix comprises ten percent of your personal credit score.

In the end, you need to have no more than one to three credit cards to avoid getting yourself into trouble. Managing them all gets much harder as you have more than three.

What Can I Do When My New Credit is Denied?

When you have new credit denied, it is possible to have the creditor reconsider your application. This starts with finding out why the application got denied in the first place. It is easy to learn why your application met with denial. Lenders have to give you an adverse action letter to explain why you were denied. The lender will also give you directions on how to get your complete free credit report (from the bureau that they used).

After you read through the adverse action letter, you might contact the creditor to request that a one of their representatives reconsider. This becomes more likely to succeed if you have new or additional information that they did not include originally in the application. Now is the time to provide it.

You might not have listed all of your eligible income sources in the application. These can include a spouse's income, government benefits, child support or alimony, or retirement savings. There could also be incorrect information on your credit report that you need to get corrected. This is a matter of opening a dispute with the credit bureau (filing online is the best way) that contains false or incomplete information.

If it is the same creditor with whom you have another account, you might ask them to move some of your existing credit line to the new account. Experts generally recommend that you wait six months between different credit card applications after credit has been denied. Every person's situation is different and so your time line could vary.

If you did not find your answer here...

Then they are probably covered within the subsequent chapters. Please look over the chapter titles to determine where your question would most likely fit. You can go straight to that chapter then and look for your question.

In the event that you do not find the answer to your question there, please feel free to contact the author directly via this website:

High Credit Score Secrets – Ask Your Question
highcreditscoresecets.com

Key Takeaways from this Chapter

Make sure that your debt balance to credit limit ratio stays low. Your goal for this figure should be no higher than 30 percent.

* * *

Opening a new credit card is an easy and effective method for increasing your available credit.

* * *

Remember that open accounts which are inactive do not hurt your credit score, but they can boost it by raising your total available credit.

* * *

By paying your bills on time every month and not using more than 30 percent of your total available credit, you will be on your way to possessing a good credit score.

* * *

Obtaining a credit card to use routinely (but responsibly) is among the fastest and most efficient means of either building up or rebuilding your credit profile and score.

* * *

Just getting your credit card balances down to 30 percent or less of your total available credit will add significant points to your credit score.

* * *

The credit utilization is the second most important factor of your credit score (at a 30 percent component).

The Benefits of Good Credit

If you lack this personal financial attribute, this will likely cost you literally tens of thousands of dollars (or possibly even hundreds of thousands of dollars) over your life time. Good credit means that you can get favourable interest rates on car loans (or leases) and mortgages on houses. Bad credit will cause you to pay sometimes exorbitant rates for these same loans.

Consider the tangible example of a thirty year fixed rate mortgage for $300,000 on a house for which you make a 20 percent down payment. With really good credit you may qualify for a 4.061 percent interest rate and an estimated monthly payment of $1,432 per month. With less good credit, you may instead get a 4.563 percent interest rate that translates to an estimated monthly payment of $1,520. The Westerra[2] team has on its website some mortgage payment examples, where you evaluate how much home you can afford.

Mortgage Payment Comparison Examples

This half a percentage point interest rate amounts to about a $90 difference in monthly payments. It may not sound like much on the surface, but when you multiply it by 360 months then you get a lifetime loan payment difference of $31,680 for the same house and mortgage.

Having good credit will measurably improve your life in so many areas. In this chapter we will consider the many personal advantages to good credit. These include psychological benefits, travel/vacation and entertainment benefits, price protection and warranties benefits, security and safety benefits, and financial benefits.

Psychological Benefits

You can not overlook or underestimate the psychological benefits that come with having good credit. If you do not have it, then every time that you apply for credit will be the next in a series of potentially embarrassing moments. This is only the beginning though.

Bad credit causes so many problems that may not immediately come to mind. If your credit is poor and you are behind on your bills, you will likely not sleep well at night because of abusive collector calls and the stress these create. You will suffer from the frustration and disruption of fighting with family members because of money problems.

With good credit, you will feel financially secure for yourself and for your family. This provides you with both the confidence and stability that you crave in life. Good credit means that you are well prepared for any unforeseen financial emergencies. When you are ready to buy a car, a house, or take out a personal loan, it will leave you in a stronger negotiating position.

Your odds of being approved for these loans and credit cards are much higher with superior credit.

Good credit can make a big difference in your professional life as well as for your personal one. Should you need to rent a house or an apartment, you will find it easier to get approved when you have good credit. You can get qualified for a mortgage loan application easier, with a potentially lower down payment, and at a more competitive interest rate that translates to tens of thousands of dollars over the life of the loan as we saw in the earlier example.

Since around half of employers now check the credit of their prospective applicants, having good credit can determine whether or not you get a competitive job. This alone could radically impact the rest of your life.

Travel, Vacation, and Entertainment Benefits

There are countless benefits to having good credit where travel and entertainment are concerned as well. If you are able to qualify for some of the best travel perks credit cards offered today (like Chase Sapphire and American Express), this can dramatically impact your vacations and even frequency of travel in your life.

Let's look at just a few examples of travel benefits that you gain with these types of valuable credit cards.

For starters, you will be able to purchase less expensive airline tickets or to receive airline upgrades using your bonus miles in the travel rewards program. This can save literally hundreds of dollars every time you use it. You also receive a range of insurances for your trip through these travel rewards credit cards and programs. It starts with free trip cancellation insurance, extends to travel accident insurance, and often includes even travel interruption insurance policies.

The peace of mind that these policies provide is invaluable and allows you to only worry about enjoying your vacation.

Another great benefit is the luggage protection policy that these rewards cards typically include. Perhaps the greatest savings with luggage comes down to the free checked bag many cards like Chase Sapphire and American Express offer. This perk is a really big deal, in particular if you are travelling as a family.

Just the savings on a free checked bag (per traveller) can amount to $50 per person, or over $200 when travelling with a family of four.

Having fantastic travel rewards credit cards from good credit can also allow you to qualify for a less expensive weekly rate for vacation rentals and even rental cars. It can give you comfortable perks like access to airport lounges (with food and drinks provided) and concierge services on your trip that ensure you get the most out of your travel. Rewards programs can provide you with significant financial savings through such perks as free hotel stays, free rounds of golf, and even free museum entrances.

You can even get Uber credit for ride shares.

A major perk for concert lovers (that cards like American Express provide) is the ability to access tickets before they go on sale to the public and to experience VIP packages. You can see how having strong reward credit cards can impact your ability to take more trips and to enjoy vacations and entertainment on a significant level.

Price Protection, Warranties, and Guarantees Benefits

This is an area of good credit benefits that many people overlook. It can save you countless headaches and frustration (when you buy things) if you have credit cards with which to purchase them. Many of today's Visa and Mastercard branded credit cards come with purchase protection like price guarantee protection.

They will also give you guaranteed returns if an item is not what you expected and extended warranties in case it stops working or breaks.

Discover cards are famous for offering quarterly cash back on everyday purchases like gas, groceries, and consumer goods. This cash back can amount to several hundred dollars per year. Over a decade of using these cash back cards you can receive back literally thousands of dollars in cash back rewards. Found money like this makes a significant impact on your ability to save and spend over time.

Security and Safety Benefits

Having good credit can save you in very practical ways too. Your financial health can be easily destroyed (or severely set back at least) by fraud. Good credit will allow you to receive credit monitoring services and alerts provided by credit cards through Bank of America, Chase, Citibank, and Barclays. You will know if someone is using your identity to open credit cards in a matter of weeks rather than accidentally finding out months or even years later when the damage can be catastrophic.

These credit cards can also provide you with money saving features like mobile phone insurance and car rental collision damage insurance. If your phone stops working within a certain period of time, the insurance will repair or replace it. When you rent a car, instead of needing to pay for the expensive rental collision insurance, you can rest confident that it will be provided by major reward credit cards such as American Express and Chase Sapphire rewards.

This savings by itself can amount to over a hundred dollars with a one to two week auto rental.

Financial Benefits

You know the benefits discussed previously in this chapter can make a difference in your peace of mind and protection. The financial advantages to having good credit can literally change your financial future. This starts with lower interest rates on loans, car loans, and credit cards and extends to better rates on car leases and mortgages to name a few.

Differences in car insurance rates can be stunning between people with good credit and poor credit.

According to the consumer website NerdWallet, drivers who possess bad credit pay an average of $1,270 more per year in car insurance premiums nationwide. This amounts to nearly $13,000 in savings (for people with good credit) over a ten year period.

The financial benefits of good credit extend to rates and limits on credit cards too. With solid credit scores, you will become eligible for higher reward, high limit credit cards that offer lower interest rates on carried balances. You will be able to participate in lucrative rewards programs that translate to double points for every dollar spent (as with Chase Sapphire).

Good credit will translate to your receiving approval with higher limits on your new cards as well. It can mean access to zero percent interest rate offers on balance transfers from credit cards like Chase Slate (Credit Karma's top pick for balance transfer offers).

Besides these balance transfer offers, you will be able to qualify to refinance your existing loans (like auto loans and mortgages) at more competitive interest rates through banks.

Having good credit can make a meaningful difference for you financially with cell phones and utilities too. When you apply to start a new cell phone contract, the mobile phone company will quietly check your credit. If your credit score is strong, then you will be able to qualify for a cell phone without having to pay a several hundred dollars security deposit.

Similarly when you apply for electric and water utilities, they will pull your credit to determine if you need to pay a $200 or higher security deposit. These security deposits are more than just a nuisance; they sap away your savings and reserves and pay you no interest.

The savings available to good credit holding individuals seem like they are endless because they really are. As you have already seen, this impacts everything from how much money you will pay to finance a house or a car (for potentially years or even decades) to whether or not you will be able to beat out the competition for a good job.

In the next chapter, we will look at fast and efficient solutions for obtaining and building up the good credit that you need to enjoy your life and future to the fullest extent.

Key Takeaways from this Chapter

Good credit means that you can get favourable interest rates on car loans (or leases) and mortgages on houses.

* * *

Good credit means that you are well prepared for any unforeseen financial emergencies.

* * *

You receive a range of insurances for your trip through these travel rewards credit cards and programs.

* * *

Visa and Mastercard branded credit cards come with purchase protection like price guarantee protection.

* * *

Good credit will allow you to receive credit monitoring services and alerts provided by credit cards through Bank of America, Chase, Citibank, and Barclays.

* * *

Lower interest rates on loans, car loans, and credit cards and extends to better rates on car leases and mortgages.

* * *

Access to zero percent interest rate offers on balance transfers from credit cards.

* * *

Differences in car insurance rates can be stunning between a good credit score and poor credit score.

CHAPTER

03

What is a Credit Score?

Introduction

Your credit score is a financial calculation of your past credit history and your capabilities of managing money. Lenders and creditors employ these scores to decide on credit approval, credit limits, and interest rates. Because the measurement of your financial health often comes down to a single number (your credit score), it is essential for you to learn how you can boost your score and to make good choices to maintain it.

Many different groups will see your credit score throughout your professional life. This starts with creditors and lenders when you apply for credit cards, car loans, and mortgages, but it does not stop there. Cell phone and utility companies considering charging you deposits, insurance companies determining your auto insurance rates, and even employers deciding who to hire (about 50 percent check prospective employees scores nowadays) will all look at your credit score.

When these groups check your scores it causes a hard inquiry that the credit bureaus will note. Checking your own score does not affect it.

Lending decisions are heavily reliant on credit scores, but it is not the only element that lenders consider. They will also look at your income, your debt to income ratio (DTI), and your past history of timely paying bills.

This is why experts recommend that you maintain a DTI of below 30 percent whenever possible.

The Different Types of Credit Scores

The topic of credit scores can be more confusing than you might think because of the simple fact that there is no single credit score. Three credit bureaus keep your credit history independently of one another (TransUnion, Experian, and Equifax) and two different companies compute credit scores.

Because there are so many different methods for scoring credit that make up your score, these numerous models will mean that your personal score can range by a number of points. This depends on whose model is being used and what kind of business is requesting it (for example, a bank, an auto dealership, or a department store).

When most people think of a credit score, they are talking about the FICO score. The Fair Isaac Company generates this. Ninety percent of lenders and creditors use FICO scores in their determinations. Yet apart from its main score, FICO has over 50 different variations of your credit score that it makes available to lenders. It means that your score will vary somewhat depending on the company asking for it and what factors were most important to them in determining your score.

As an example, a department store FICO score they generate for you could be a little better than your FICO score sent to a bank deciding on approving you for a car loan. Both of these will be somewhat different from your insurance-based FICO score. All of these will be a little different from your mortgage loan FICO score.

The other main credit scoring company produces Vantage Scores. Vantage was created as an alliance by the three main credit bureaus to try to reconcile differences between the various bureaus and to standardize the results. While Vantage's prominence has risen since the creation of the company in 2006, their Vantage Score is still less important by far than your FICO score.

All else being equal, you want to have good credit scores generated by both FICO and Vantage Score.

Each of the three principle credit reporting bureaus also generates its own credit scores. These will vary somewhat as some creditors and lenders may not report your credit and payment history to all three bureaus. A lender or creditor can choose to request one or more of these reports to ascertain whether or not to extend you credit or a loan in determining your credit worthiness. One thing that has made understanding your credit score easier is that Vantage Score adjusted its credit score range to match that of FICO.

Your credit score will range from 300 to 850 with either company[3].

These credit scoring models are created using data from the credit bureaus to analyze your worthiness to receive and ability to manage credit. The agencies choose important characteristics contained in your patterns for paying credit, analyze these, then compute a credit score for you.

They calculate your scores looking at your timeliness of payments, your payment record, numbers and totals of debt, numbers of credit cards that you have, and any credit charge offs.

Different weightings will be assigned to each component in the formula of the model to assign a credit score dependent on this evaluation. This number will range from a possible low of 300 to a highest possible score of 850.

Lenders then employ these credit scores to ascertain the level of risk in issuing you a loan, your loan terms, and its interest rate. With a higher credit score, your loan terms will be more advantageous. You can see why it is important to understand your credit score model and how you can improve this. Next we will look at the two main models that FICO and Vantage Score use so that you can grasp how they judge each component category.

The FICO Scoring Model

FICO holds the distinction of most reliable scoring model thanks in no small part to its longstanding track record. Fair Isaac Company began computing these scores back in 1989. They have since revised the algorithms a number of times in the past over three decades to adjust for shifting factors so that they produce continuously dependable credit scores.

As we noted earlier, the traditional FICO score model will produce a score for you from 300 to 850. Scores of less than 600 equate to poor. If your score is higher than 740 then this is deemed to be excellent.

The ranges in between 600 and 740 mean from average to above average credit worthiness.

In 2014, FICO introduced its FICO 9 scoring model. The primary revision in this model was to reduce the importance of unpaid medical bills. The reasoning behind this is that medical debts that are not paid are not truly financial health indicators.

You might be waiting for insurance to pay a medical bill or simply be unaware that a medical bill had been given over to a collection agency. For some people, this important change allowed their credit score to increase by up to 25 points.

Other changes in 2017 stopped collectors from reporting late medical debts that were not yet 180 days delinquent. Year 2017 also saw the three credit reporting bureaus drop all of their data on civil judgments and the tax lien records from their files. FICO reported that this helped the scores of around six percent of consumers.

Before FICO 9 came out, FICO 8 (that the company developed in 2009) was the standard credit score version. FICO 8 remains the most commonly utilized score of the lending industry. FICO 8's distinguishing features were to penalize you for charging near your total credit limit each month and to provide clemency if you had only a single late payment of over 30 days.

It is worth noting that each time FICO releases an updated version on its scoring models, lenders may keep the version they are using or upgrade. FICO 8 has remained the overwhelming favorite simply because it costs so much to upgrade to the new model. There are lenders still using even FICO 5 models.

You can ask your lender which model they are using when you go through the application process.

FICO scores typically do not change that much over the short term. The exception is if you start missing payments or showing charge offs and defaults. Not everyone has a FICO score either. If you do not have credit, you will fall into the category of what experts call "credit invisible."

You must have six months of payments reported to the credit bureaus in order to have a FICO score.

The second main scoring model in use today is the Vantage Score model. The three credit bureaus Experian, Equifax, and TransUnion made a rare show of unity back in 2006 when they decided that they would create a competitor to FICO in an effort to standardize credit scores. The end result was to increase the number of credit scores available to lenders and creditors.

Vantage Score's model considers similar data to FICO but weights them differently. They look at on time payment of your bills, maintaining lower credit card balances, and taking on too many new credit obligations to compile their score. Vantage's primary advantage for people who are new to credit is that they can generate a score for you in as little as two months from your first reported credit card payments.

FICO scores are different from generic credit scores. They apply a proprietary set of algorithms to come up with your credit risk using the information found within your personal credit reports. Other companies will often pattern their credit scores to look as close to a FICO credit score as they can, but as FICO notes[4], this can result in scores that are even 100 points apart from the gold standard in the industry.

Even a couple of points can determine whether you get a favorable interest rate and set of terms (saving you as much as thousands of dollars over the term of the loan or credit). In the next section we will look at how the two principle scoring companies come up with your credit scores specifically.

How Are My Credit Scores Calculated?

The FICO Scoring Algorithm

Irrespective of the FICO model a lender or credit uses, five factors generally impact the FICO classic score they use to come up with your credit score. These are payment history, credit utilization, credit history, credit types, and new credit. Some categories also have sub-categories within them. We will go through each of these components next.

1. Payment History

Your payment history comprises 35 percent of your score, making it the most important single component in determining your credit score. By making your monthly payments in a timely fashion each month and not showing bad public records of lawsuits, foreclosure, or bankruptcy you will score well here. Late payments detract from your score.

Your score is more heavily penalized the later your payment is (two months penalizes worse than one month).

2. Credit Utilization

The second most important category with FICO scores is your credit utilization, amounting to 30 percent of your total score. The key here is to stay as far away from using all of your credit limit, regardless of whether you will pay the full bill when it arrives. FICO wants to see you with 30 percent or less of your available credit used.

This means that you should not spend over $150 each month on a $500 credit card limit.

3. Credit History

The next most important factor is credit history for 15 percent of your total score. By this FICO means the amount of time you have possessed your credit cards. The greater amount of time you have had your first one and the longer your average credit account history, the higher your score in this category will be.

4. Credit Types

Your credit mix amounts to 10 percent. FICO is interested in the different types of credit that you possess (including credit cards, mortgage, car loans, utilities, store accounts) and the way that you pay them on time. It will help you have a better score if you count a range of different loans and credit cards on your report.

The key is not to over-apply for these accounts in a short time frame. Credit bureaus interpret this as a warning sign that you could be desperate to get more credit.

5. New Credit

New credit is the final category with FICO, and it equates to 10 percent of their calculation. The more cards you apply for at once, the worse your score in this category will be. They see it as a possibility that you are attempting to juggle your debt using new credit cards, a definite negative.

It is better for your score to spread out your applications as much as possible.

The Vantage Score Algorithm

Vantage Score is using similar criteria to weigh your credit worthiness as does FICO. The primary differences are the weighting that they place on the different components and the fact that they pull data from all three credit reporting bureaus in determining your score. We look at their six scoring components next.

1. Payment History – Highest Weighting

The top forecaster of risk for you with Vantage Score is your payment history. Their model assigns a 40 percent weighting to this, making it twice as important as their next most important category, or as important as the second and third categories combined.

Late payments must be avoided at all costs. These can stay on your credit report for as long as seven years.

2. Age/Type of Credit – Extreme Weighting

This category is the combination of credit history length and your kinds of credit. If you are able to make on time payments on a five year auto loan while you are paying 30 year mortgage payments and monthly credit card bills, then Vantage Score considers you exceptional in this category.

It counts for 21 percent, making it the second most important part of the algorithm.

3. Credit Utilization – Extreme Weighting

To come up with this figure, you simply divide your total balances by your available credit. You should maintain this level at less than 30 percent. Ten percent is even better.

4. Total Balances – Medium Weighting

Vantage Score gives 11 percent weighting to your total debt category (whether it is current or delinquent). By lowering your total debt, you will achieve a higher score in this category.

5. Recent Behavior – Low Weighting

This category gets five percent. It looks into how many recently opened accounts you have as well as the quantities of hard inquiries. It is considered higher risk when you have a larger number of hard inquiries since you could be taking on significantly more debt.

6. Available Credit – Extremely Low Weighting

This category counts for three percent. Available credit refers to the amount in credit that you have available for use at any given point. The more credit you have available, the more points they will assign you in this least important category.

Credit Karma is the biggest name using Vantage Score's model these days. They offer a completely free service (giving you your credit report and a credit score) that is subscribed to by over a hundred million consumers. You can also get credit monitoring from them.

Vantage Score is also on revised versions now. In 2017, they changed their model in the trended data. Now if you are making larger payments to pay down your debt, then you will get more points than an individual who only makes the minimum monthly payments and one who is gradually increasing credit card debt.

Something else that sets Vantage Score apart from FICO and other credit scoring models is that they ignore collections if they are under $250. They also provide dispensation for people who have suffered from natural disasters. Vantage Score also gives a letter grade of A through F alongside their credit score so that consumers are better able to comprehend what their credit score signifies.

Several elements are not covered by your credit scores. One of these is if you have been turned down for credit. Another is your marital status. Your income does not show on your credit reports either. Since this information does not appear in your credit reports, it is not directly reflected in your credit scores.

What Influences My Credit Score the Most?

There are a number of factors that impact your credit score. It is helpful to consider the ones that influence it the most so you can target these and improve your personal score. Inquiries are an area that you can easily address. Whenever you apply for credit or a loan, the creditor or lender will do what is called a hard inquiry on your credit report. While one or two of these will not have major impact, a number of them at a time can cost you points in the new credit category.

Checking your own credit through a consumer service like Credit Karma or by requesting your full credit reports does not harm your score.

Bankruptcy dramatically impacts your credit score, and it can be more damaging than any other single factor. The two types of personal bankruptcy are Chapter 7 and Chapter 13. The primary difference is that a successful Chapter 7 will discharge your debts, while Chapter 13 involves a repayment schedule of from three to five years.

In both cases, bankruptcy commonly does not fall off of your credit report for seven years after it is completed (though it can remain for up to 10 years). This makes Chapter 13 bankruptcy longer lasting and more damaging as your discharge is delayed by years.

FICO scores penalize people filing for bankruptcy with stronger credit more severely than those with only average credit.

Income does not show up on your credit report, so it does not directly impact your credit score. If you apply for credit or loans, the lender will ask your income and use this to figure up your debt to income ratio.

Your debt to income ratio should ideally be less than 30 percent.

This is also the percent you should keep as a maximum with your credit usage every month. Higher numbers will cost you in the credit utilization component of your FICO score.

Leasing a car will usually not impact your credit score any differently than financing a car in an auto loan. If you make the payments on time every month, it will build or rebuild your credit as the payments get reported to the three credit bureaus. Paying off a lease early can damage your credit, as the account gets reported as closed to the credit bureaus, something that they misinterpret as having settled a debt for less than you owed on it (even though you will pay more in penalties to close it out early[5]).

Refinancing is another area of which you should be wary. If you pursue cash out refinance, this can have two negative effects on your credit score. First, you are replacing an older loan with a new loan, hurting your average age of credit history FICO component. Secondly, if it is a larger loan, then this will negatively raise your credit utilization ratio.

Because this utilization ratio comprises 30 percent of your FICO credit score, you should be careful about increasing it through a refinancing. With any refinancing, be careful not to do it too often (which looks like you do not honor your contracts) or to shop around for rates much (which causes multiple hard hits on your credit at once and can cost you points[6]).

Some good news for you who owe the IRS money is that tax liens no longer show up on your credit reports. Experian reports that this decision was made in 2017, and all tax liens were removed from the three credit reporting bureaus by April of 2018. The result is that tax liens do not any longer have an impact on your credit scores[7].

Your Most Important Lesson to Learn About Credit Scores

The top two components of your personal score are timely payment history (making up 35 percent) and credit card utilization (amounting to 30 percent). You should avoid delinquencies, charge offs, and especially bankruptcy if at all possible to preserve this most important category of payment history.

Also you need to make serious efforts to keep your credit card utilization below 30 percent so that you can attain a good score in the second most important category.

Now that you know all about what precisely makes up your credit score, it is time to get proactive about boosting it. We will look at the top 15 ways in the next chapter.

Use the Free Credit Score Simulator

Estimate the change of your credit score by choosing various financial scenarios. No signup or account needed!

https://highcreditscoresecrets.com/free-credit-score-simulator

How to Use the Credit Score Simulator

Based on the average US customer credit score we have set the initial start score to 690, which is in the 'Good' range.

Please adjust your current credit status first if it's not in the 'Good' range. Then add your total credit limit as well as your current balance. Proceed by clicking on the various questions and check with different financial scenarios.

It's best practise to simulate only one change at a time. The more changes you simulate at once the less accurate the result.

How to Improve Your Score

These 5 factors make up your credit score:

- Credit Inquiries – 10%
- Type of Credit – 10%
- Credit Longevity – 15%
- Credit Balances – 30%
- Payment History – 35%

You will find all relevant credit related information in High Credit Score Secrets. This practical compendium reveals over 50 ways you can boost your credit rating. Understand the exact mathematical algorithm that all 3 major credit bureaus use to calculate your credit score.

Learn what actions you can take to improve your credit score and what behavior will demote it.

Disclaimer

Currently, the FICO Score 9 is the most commonly used credit score model. We have adapted the FICO score scale, but the calculation model we use differs from the FicoScore and VantageScore. However, our calculations are close enough and they will give you a good overview of what will happen to your score if certain financial situations change.

Our tool is not capable of providing exact estimates and you should not make any financial decisions based on the output from our simulator. If you find any problems with this credit simulator, or if you have suggestions please don't hesitate to contact me.

Key Takeaways from this Chapter

Your credit score will range from 300 to 850 with FICO or Vantage.

* * *

You must have six months of payments reported to the credit bureaus in order to have a FICO score.

* * *

Your score is more heavily penalized the later your payment is (two months penalizes worse than one month).

* * *

Late payments must be avoided at all costs. These can stay on your credit report for as long as seven years.

* * *

Age and type of credit counts for 21 percent, making it the second most important part of the algorithm.

* * *

Checking your own credit through a consumer service like Credit Karma or by requesting your full credit reports does not harm your score.

* * *

Your debt to income ratio should ideally be less than 30 percent.

* * *

Make serious efforts to keep your credit card utilization below 30 percent so that you can attain a good score in the second most important category.

Where Do I Stand With My Credit Score?

Credit scores come in a range of 300 to 850. In that vast range you find everyone in the country who has a credit score. Where are you standing with your FICO and VantageScore credit scores these days? We will look at these numbers in this chapter.

Average FICO Score Statistics[8]

The average FICO score for American consumers is 695 (as of April 2019). This is actually a good credit score. Poor scores are those below 550 with FICO. Nearly 12 percent of Americans possess a credit score that is 549 or lower per FICO. They are the sub prime borrowers.

Looking at the other end of the range, some US citizen actually possess an over 800 FICO credit score. These fortunate individuals (with an 800 to 850 score) comprise over 20 percent of the population. These are the super prime borrowers.

It is hard, although not impossible, to have a perfect 850 FICO credit score. This rarest of credit scores belongs to under one percent of the entire population.

Average VantageScore Statistics

At this same time in 2019, the average American possessed a VantageScore of 673. Millenials (aged 22 to 35) boasted a VantageScore of only 634. The next category of adults aged from 35 to 51 were slightly higher on average with a Gen X VantageScore amounting to 655. Baby Boomers of the 52 to 70 year age group boasted an impressive average 700 VantageScore. The Silent Generation of seniors aged over 70 did the best, holding average VantageScores of 730[9].

Gender's Impact Your Credit Score

In a word, yes your gender does impact your credit scores. The reason has nothing to do with secret discrimination though. The Board of Governors of the Federal Reserve conducted a survey analyzing over 10 years of data obtained from TransUnion and Mintel.

They gathered data on over 4,000 single women and over 3,700 single men aged 21 to 40. Head Economist Geng Li who wrote the report discovered that women had lower credit scores on average than men. The average women's VantageScore in the 21 to 30 age group was 762 versus the men of the same group's 768. In the group of from 31 to 40, men boasted 793 to women's 785.

Though women boasted fewer credit inquiries and a longer credit history established, the women were also more likely to consistently carry larger amounts of debt leading to higher credit utilization ratios and to fall into late payments and delinquent accounts than the men in either age group.

The two highest component categories of the scoring models hurt women more than men as a result and led to lower female credit scores in general. Yet it is worth nothing that the disparity was about one percent apart only.

Overview of Credit Scores by Year, Age, Income, and State

It is good to know where you stand versus your peers in credit scores. I have gathered this information in this final section. Below I compare average credit scores based on year and age, income, and by state.

Average Credit Scores by Year and Age

By age, there is a surprising spread of credit scores. The following table shows the differences in averages:

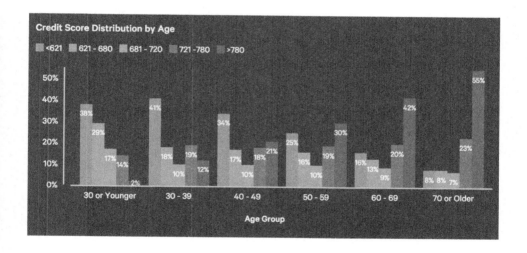

Average Credit Scores by Income

Credit scores by income varied significantly from the bottom earners to the top ones. The lowest income category with less than 50 percent of the median family income had a 664 score. Moderate income individuals with a from 51 percent to 79 percent of the MFI had 716, a significantly better credit score.

The middle income group of from 80 percent to 119 percent of the MFI possessed a score of 753. Finally, the top earners with over 120 percent of the MFI counted on an average credit score of 775, per Lending Tree and Value Penguin's data and graphs[10].

Average Credit Scores By State

By state, there was a somewhat surprising range of credit scores. This table below shows the distribution of scores per state:

Rank	State	ø Score	ø Cards	ø Balance
35	Alaska	668	2.9	$8,515
48	Alabama	654	2.69	$5,961
43	Arkansas	657	2.76	$5,660
34	Arizona	669	3.04	$6,389
24	California	680	3.23	$6,481
15	Colorado	688	3.13	$6,718
12	Connecticut	690	3.23	$7,258
33	District of Columbia	670	2.98	$6,963
31	Delaware	672	3.13	$6,366
35	Florida	668	3.19	$6,388
48	Georgia	654	2.97	$6,675
10	Hawaii	693	3.25	$6,981

Rank	State	ø Score	ø Cards	ø Balance
8	Iowa	695	2.67	$5,155
23	Idaho	681	2.88	$5,817
21	Illinois	683	3.14	$6,410
37	Indiana	667	2.77	$5,581
24	Kansas	680	2.82	$6,082
39	Kentucky	663	2.78	$5,555
50	Louisiana	650	2.77	$6,074
5	Massachusetts	699	3.21	$6,327
31	Maryland	672	3.16	$7,043
13	Maine	689	2.91	$5,784
29	Michigan	677	2.91	$5,622
1	Minnesota	709	2.97	$5,911
30	Missouri	675	2.91	$5,897
51	Mississippi	647	2.57	$5,421
13	Montana	689	2.87	$5,845
38	North Carolina	666	2.95	$6,117
6	North Dakota	697	2.9	$5,511
8	Nebraska	695	2.83	$5,630
3	New Hampshire	701	3.1	$6,490
20	New Jersey	686	3.49	$7,151
41	New Mexico	659	2.79	$6,317
47	Nevada	655	3.18	$6,401
15	New York	688	3.34	$6,671

Rank	State	ø Score	ø Cards	ø Balance
27	Ohio	678	3.02	$5,843
45	Oklahoma	656	2.71	$6,296
15	Oregon	688	2.95	$6,012
18	Pennsylvania	687	3.07	$6,146
18	Rhode Island	687	3.26	$6,375
43	South Carolina	657	2.9	$6,157
4	South Dakota	700	2.8	$5,692
40	Tennessee	662	2.77	$5,975
45	Texas	656	3.06	$6,902
21	Utah	683	2.95	$5,960
24	Virginia	680	3.08	$7,161
2	Vermont	702	2.86	$5,924
10	Washington	693	2.99	$6,592
7	Wisconsin	696	2.8	$5,363
42	West Virginia	658	2.76	$5,547
27	Wyoming	678	2.81	$6,245

Average Credit Scores of Home Buyers

The average homebuyer had a high credit score of 728. This was a little bit higher than the national average in general. Of more than 85,000 applicants for mortgages which the Federal Reserve surveyed, only 6.8 percent possessed a score under 620.

The U.S. Federal Reserve Bank published a credit report on home buyers in 2010. The data considered minority groups versus whites as well. Every group surveyed except for African American consumers possessed credit score averages higher than 700.

Asian borrowers were the most fortunate, with an average high of 745 in FICO credit scores. Non-hispanic white had 734 average scores. Hispanics had 701 scores on average[11].

Key Takeaways from this Chapter

The average FICO score for American consumers is 695 (as of April 2019).

* * *

At this same time in 2019, the average American possessed a VantageScore of 673.

* * *

The average homebuyer had a high credit score of 728.

* * *

The lowest income category with less than 50 percent of the median family income had a 664 score.

* * *

Moderate income individuals with a from 51 percent to 79 percent of the MFI had 716, a significantly better credit score.

* * *

The middle income group of from 80 percent to 119 percent of the MFI possessed a score of 753.

* * *

The top earners with over 120 percent of the MFI counted on an average credit score of 775.

What Positively Influences Your Credit Score?

Top 15 Ways to Positively Impact Your Credit Score

1. Choose a Secured Credit Card and Pay it Off Frequently

Secured credit cards are great tools to help you build up (or rebuild) credit with the three credit reporting agencies Experian, Equifax, and TransUnion. By making a deposit of typically $250-$500, you gain a credit line of the same amount (or sometimes higher).

You should use the card for purchases then pay it off as often as possible. This will establish good timely paying history, which gives you points in that most important category of payment history (counting for 35 percent of your credit score).

Remember to keep your credit utilization on the card to less than 30 percent (for the credit utilization component of 30 percent of your credit score)

2. Get More Credit

If you do this judiciously, it can positively impact your credit score. The reason is because more available credit can translate to a lower total credit utilization amount (30 percent of your credit score). The key with this is not to apply for too much credit all at once, as this creates hard inquiries on your credit reports (too many negatively impact your new credit component of 10 percent).

Try to get different kinds of credit since this impresses the credit bureaus. Store accounts, credit cards, auto loans, and mortgages all contribute to the credit mix category (counting for 10 percent of your score).

3. Raise Your Credit Limits

The more available credit you have, the better you look to the credit scoring algorithms. Your ultimate goal is to keep your credit utilization down to less than 30 percent. This is easier to do when you have $2,000 in total available credit rather than only $1,000. Higher credit limits that you do not overuse show the reporting bureaus that you are more capable of successfully managing debt and credit.

The credit utilization category is the second most important with FICO and a close third for Vantage Scoring models.

4. Charge Small Amounts to an Inactive Credit Card

If you allow months or perhaps even years to lapse between charges on an inactive credit card, the issuer will likely close it. This would hurt you in two ways. It would reduce your total available credit, increasing your total credit utilization (the 30 percent component).

If you have $2,000 charged on $6,000 in available credit, this is 33 percent utilization. Should one of your creditors close a $1,500 card that you do not use then your utilization increases to $2,000 over $4,500, a far higher utilization rate of 44 percent.

Lower is always better with this utilization number. The 33 percent utilization is almost at the maximum level the scoring models want to see, while 44 percent is definitely considered high and is penalized.

Having an inactive account closed would also lower your credit accounts average age (the credit history component counts for 15 percent). Avoiding this danger is easy. Take any inactive credit cards out when you shop to make at least small routine charges to them. This will keep your creditor happy and improve your credit score[12].

5. Pay Off High Interest Credit Accounts First

If you are carrying balances on your credit cards, there is a definite strategy to smartly paying them down. You should always attack the highest interest rate balances first. Higher interest charges are increasing the total debt you have each month, damaging your credit utilization component.

Paying these down first will reduce the amount of time it takes to get your debt erased and under control.

6. Get a Credit Builder Loan

One of the easier ways to improve your credit score is by varying your credit mix. You can get more points in this component that counts for 10 percent by applying for a credit building loan. Be sure you make all of your loan payments on time, and this will also help out your most important component of timely payment history (35 percent of credit score).

7. Pay Off A Debt

By eliminating one of your debts, you successfully reduce your credit utilization component that counts for 30 percent of your score. This also raises your available credit, a component that Vantage Scoring model considers. It will give you additional points in your most important payment history component as well.

8. Remove Recent Late Payments

Creditor bureaus are not required to remove late payments unless they are reported mistakenly in error. You can always approach your creditor and ask them to take off a late payment from your credit report though. You can do this over the phone or in writing.

If the creditor removes the late information, then it will disappear from your credit reports.

Be sure to provide any good explanations for why you were late. It might be that you suffered a financial hardship like going to the hospital or a natural disaster. The late payment might not have been your fault (and you have documentation to prove the bank error or other cause).

If you always pay your bills in a timely fashion, explain to them that it was an inadvertent, one time mistake.

When you have something to offer the creditor in return for helping you out, this may increase their willingness. You can offer to pay down (or off) a loan in exchange. You lose a number of points for a late payment in the payment history component, so anything you can do to get this removed can help you significantly[13].

9. Remove a Collection Account

Collection accounts equate to charge offs. These cause serious damage to your credit score. You can contact the original creditor and offer to pay them the full balance in exchange for them retracting it from collections. They may be willing to accommodate you to have the debt paid off. At the very least, they will have to report your debt as paid in full when you cover it.

10. Pay Off a Past Due Balance

Past due balances negatively impact your credit score in the most crucial payment history category (35 percent). The longer they are negative for, the worse they harm your score. The balance will show as current once you bring the account up to date. Paying it off will help your score to improve even more.

If a past due balance is only an isolated event, FICO will not penalize you for it under their newest algorithm versions FICO 8 and FICO 9.

11. Pay More Than One Time in a Billing Cycle

Paying more frequently (than once in a billing cycle) will help to keep your credit utilization amount down. The reason is that your statement balance is the one reported to the credit bureaus. By reducing this number, you can effectively lower your credit utilization.

Remember that your goal is to keep this number to less than 30 percent and ideally under 10 percent (for 30 percent of your credit score component).

Making extra payments will also help you to pay off any balance you are carrying sooner and reduce significantly the amount of finance charges you are assessed.

12. Dispute Any Credit Report Errors

Credit report errors are a fact of life. They can have an impact on your credit score needlessly. The answer is to frequently check your own credit reports for accuracy. If you see mistakes, go online to the credit reporting bureau website right away and file a dispute. It can take the bureaus up to a month to investigate and correct these errors, so do not put it off.

The websites for this are TransUnion disputes, Equifax disputes, and Experian disputes.

13. Pay Down Revolving Balances to Less than 30 Percent

The credit scoring models are heavily concerned with how much of your available credit you utilize (counting for 30 percent). They want to see less than 30 percent used. If you have $5,000 in available credit, then this means keeping a balance of under $1,500 at the end of each month. You can pay down one or more of your balances even before the statement is issued to accomplish this.

Ideally you should try to keep this credit utilization number to even less than 10 percent for maximum points in the category.

14. Use an Eligibility Checker

When you are considering applying for new credit, you want to be careful to avoid too many hard inquiries on your credit reports. This is a component of your score that counts for 10 percent. The way to shop around without harming your credit score is to use an eligibility checker before applying. This way you will be able to reduce the number of creditors to whom you apply for credit.

Tools like the eligibility calculator at:

https://www.moneysavingexpert.com/eligibility/credit-cards/

will even give you a percentage chance of being approved for the cards you query about without needing to have any hard inquiries on your reports. They also help you to choose the cards that are best for your personal circumstances to narrow down the crowded credit card field.

15. Use a Co-Signer

If you are new to a credit history or trying to rebuild a damaged one, a simple way to get better loan and credit card approvals is by bring into play a co-signer. A family member or friend can help you with this if they have strong credit. You receive the benefit of having the loan or credit on your credit report by "borrowing" from their good credit. It will also help you to benefit from more advantageous terms and lower interest rates on the loan or credit.

Additional Tips to Help Raise Your Score

Besides the top 15 ways to improve your credit score, there are a number of other useful tips you can follow to raise this measure of personal financial health. Some of these are simple things that you might not consider otherwise.

Check if You Are Linked to Another Person

Sometimes another individual's credit gets tied to your own by mistake. This is easy to correct by filing disputes with the credit reporting bureaus. It can have a massive impact on your score if this individual's credit is poor.

Use Your Secured Credit Card Sparingly at First

You want to keep your credit utilization category low. This gives you more points in this second most important category. The credit card company is also more likely to raise your limit or refund your deposit when they see this type of responsible financial behaviour.

Check for Fraudulent Activity and Fix It

Fraud affected 46 percent of Americans over the past five years, according to electronic payment systems firm ACI Worldwide[14]. If you spot fraudulent activity on your credit report, you need to address this immediately before it becomes more damaging. Requesting a credit freeze is the fastest way to stop the problem from getting any worse. Then you can set about disputing the fraudulent activity.

Move Less Often

Taking on new mortgages continuously can affect you negatively in several ways. You never pay down your mortgage loan. Your credit history average is shortened with each new mortgage as well. By staying in your home and paying your mortgage on time every month, you show the stability and financial responsibility that the credit scoring models love.

Leave Accounts Open

It can be tempting to close credit cards that you do not use, but this harms you in two categories. Your credit utilization will rise if you lose available credit. This is the second most important category comprising 30 percent of your score. Also closing accounts lowers your average account credit history, a component that makes up 15 percent of your score. Keep these accounts open, charge small amounts from time to time, and then pay them off every month to improve your score.

Take an Auto Loan and a Mortgage

The credit mix category amounts to 10 percent of your score. Creditors like to see different kinds of credit that you are keeping up with on your reports. Two categories they especially like are mortgages and car loans. Having these will give you a number of points in this category and also a stronger payment history category (the most important component).

Pay Your Rent on Time Every Month

You can ask your property management company to report your monthly rent payments to the credit bureaus. This will improve your payment history category that is the most important component. If your landlord does not offer this service, try signing up for an electronic rent payment service which will guarantee reporting to all three major credit bureaus. Some of the big names in this industry are Rent Track, Pay Lease, eRent Payment, Pay Your Rent, and Clear Now.

Pay Your Cell Phone and Utility Bills on Time

Most utilities and cell phone providers will report your payment history to the credit bureaus. This is a good way to build up new credit or rebuild damaged credit. It counts towards the most important component of payment history.

Get a Personal or Secured Loan

Another way to improve your credit mix category (10 percent of your score) is by taking out either a personal or secured loan. This will give you another form of credit to show on your report. It could add several key points to your FICO or Vantage Scoring scores.

Become an Authorized User

For individuals just starting out with credit, this is a great way for you to establish a payment history. Your parents or a trusted friend can make you an authorized user on one of their credit cards. With each timely payment, you will benefit in the key category of rent payment history. It will also give you a credit utilization component, the second most important category.

Get Credit for the Bills You Pay

Make sure that all bills you pay are reporting to one or more of the credit reporting bureaus. You can ask companies to do this if they are not already. Timely rent payment is a very good one to have on your report.

Obtain Store Credit Cards or Student Credit Cards

Another great way to improve your credit mix component (10 percent of credit scores) is by obtaining store credit. For people who are newly establishing a credit profile, getting a store credit card or student credit card are two of the easier ways to get those all important first accounts approved and open.

Register on the Electoral Roll

This adds another source for your address and contact details to your credit report. Odd as it may seem, it does increase your credit score too, according to Experian[15].

Key Takeaways from this Chapter

Keep your credit utilization on the card to less than 30 percent (for the credit utilization component of 30 percent of your credit score).

* * *

The credit utilization category is the second most important with FICO and a close third for Vantage Scoring models.

* * *

If a past due balance is only an isolated event, FICO will not penalize you for it under their newest algorithm versions FICO 8 and FICO 9.

* * *

Making extra payments will also help you to pay off any balance you are carrying sooner and reduce significantly the amount of finance charges you are assessed.

* * *

Ideally you should try to keep the credit utilization number to even less than 10 percent for maximum points in the category.

* * *

If you spot fraudulent activity requesting a credit freeze is the fastest way to stop the problem from getting any worse. Then you can set about disputing the fraudulent activity.

* * *

Keep accounts open, charge small amounts from time to time, and then pay them off every month to improve your score.

What Negatively Influences
Your Credit Score?

Introduction

Now that you know the top factors that positively influence your credit score, it is time to consider the ones that most negatively impact it. Knowledge is power, and being aware of these actions will help you to avoid costly credit score mistakes. We look at the top 10 negative influences to your score here next. But first, here is some good news regarding government and private liens.

Private and Government Liens and Judgments No Longer Impact Credit Reports/Scores!

Credit mistakes to avoid used to include government liens, until 2015 when the three major credit bureaus Experian, Equifax, and TransUnion banded together and ruled that they would no longer consider tax liens on credit reports towards credit scores. This initiative was a component of the NCAP National Consumer Assistance Plan that took effect in 2017 and 2018.

Other liens are now similarly treated. Property liens no longer influence your credit score as they are not included on credit reports as of 2017/2018. Such property liens could also encompass a judgement lien against a property you own.

If you lose a civil court case and owe other parties money for unpaid medical bills, child support, or credit card bills, this will no longer appear on your credit report nor influence your credit score any longer[16]. It will not prevent the other party from attempting to recover the owed money however.

In the past, civil judgments (debts that you owed because of a court ruling) would have shown up on your credit report. As of 2018, Experian reports that the three major credit bureaus no longer list any judgments on anyone's credit reports and do not factor them into credit scoring models therefore. This relief applies to all negative public records information except for bankruptcies[17].

The Top 10 Negative Influencers of Your Credit Score

1. Collections Accounts

Collections occur when you have a debt that you have not paid in a timely manner. When you fall substantially behind in delinquency on a bill like a credit card or medical bill, the original creditor will usually write off the debt as a total loss. They then sell it out to a collection agency. It is then entirely up to the collection agency to try to get the money that you owe back.

Not every lender or creditor has the same policy on this action. A great number of credit cards send out the 180 day delinquent accounts to collectors. At this point, either they or the collection agency will report your account as "in collections" to the major three credit bureaus. This will cause you to have a "collection" notation on your credit reports.

The original creditor may or may not alert you to the fact that they are sending your account out to collections.

Once you suffer an in collection account on your credit report, you can anticipate your credit score plunging. The number of points such a collection account will impact your score depends on how high your credit score proves to be when it becomes reported as a collection account.

A correspondingly higher credit score will lose more points in general.

The amount of the account in collection will also determine how big an impact this status has on your credit score. If your original debt amount was under $100, the collection account may appear on your credit reports but not much harm your score (or even hurt it at all with Vantage Scoring's model for under $250 collections accounts).

Some of the credit scoring models distinguish between the various kinds of debt, like non medical or medical, while others will discard penalties for collections accounts that you have paid off[18].

2. Foreclosures and Short Sales

Foreclosures and short sales have to do with mortgages on which you fall behind. The bank has the right to foreclose on your property if you become seriously delinquent. You could also arrange a short sale with the bank to repay part of the loan and settle it. Both of these impact your credit score in several meaningful ways.

Yet short sales done properly will create a less negative effect on your personal credit score than an all out foreclosure will.

Foreclosures can have a devastating impact on your credit score. For starters, it will stay on your credit report for a full 10 years, though the impact will be gradually less as it gets older.

The late payments that led to the foreclosure cause a significant negative effect on your credit score. According to FICO, foreclosures will cause an estimated drop of from 175 to 300 points in your score[19].

Short sales have a considerably smaller impact on your score. This is a more difficult procedure as it requires approval from the mortgage lender who is involved. You will have to give the lender an application detailed with information on your financials.

If you can arrange a short sale with your lender without missing any mortgage payments, it will reduce the negative impact on your credit score.

Also, you should negotiate so that your lender reports to the credit bureaus that your short sale was paid in full. It will make a considerable difference in the way it is interpreted from your credit report.

If you can not get a fast approval of such a short sale from your lender, you may be forced into missing payments on your mortgage. This would cause your score more harm as timely payment history amounts to 35 percent of your FICO credit scoring component. The lender could also determine that you do not meet their qualifications for a short sale, which would then leave you with either finding a way to hold onto the house or letting it fall into foreclosure eventually.

3. Bill Payment History of Late Payments

There is no larger single element that impacts your credit score than timely payments (amounting to 35 percent of your credit scoring model). This means that missing a payment and having it marked as late to the credit reporting bureaus will hurt, sometimes quite a lot.

A late payment that is reported as 30 days or more past due could crash your credit score by up to 100 points.

If your credit is without blemish, it might cause this amount of a drop. When your score is already lower, it will not affect it as much, but it will still damage it[20].

4. Increased Debt to Credit Ratio

The total debt that you possess remains the second largest factor in determining your personal credit score. As a 30 percent component of your credit score, you can not afford to abuse this ratio. Credit scoring models look at this credit utilization (the ratio of your credit card balance to your total credit limit) on every one of your cards as well as your total credit utilization for all accounts.

The higher these balances are compared to your credit limits, the more damage this does to your personal score.

The worst possible thing you can show in this category is over limit or maxed out card balances (amounting to 100 percent or higher utilization).

Remember that credit scores also consider the proximity of your loan balances to original loan amounts. This is why paying down loan balances will help your credit score.

The opposite is true too. If you carry large amounts of debt (in particular credit card debt), this will harm your credit score and be damaging in your efforts to get new loans and credit card approvals (or to increase your credit limits).

Your debt to income ratio might be low, but if your credit utilization ratio is high, this will negatively impact your total score. It could subsequently cause you to be denied obtaining credit. The credit scoring models want to see no higher than 30 percent debt to credit ratio and prefer 10 percent in an ideal world[21].

5. Repossessions

Repossession occurs if you miss multiple loan payments that cause you to default on your car loan. The statutes in most states today permit your creditor to assume possession of the car (from a delinquent auto loan) whenever it is convenient for them. Repossession is an especially bad mark on a credit report as it remains for up to seven years and can cause you a 100 point credit score drop.

Repossessions harm your credit in three meaningful ways.

This starts with late payments. These cause negative effects on your credit report for up to seven years by themselves. Once your car has been repossessed, the three main credit bureaus will likely include notations that your car has been repossessed for up to seven long years.

Collections efforts to recover money you still owe on the loan after they repossess and sell your vehicle will also show on your report for as long as seven years. This is the case even if you pay off the debt later[22].

The best way to avoid going through the damage of repossession is to stay in contact with your lender once you fall behind on payments. You may be able to arrange an easier and longer repayment schedule if you have suffered from financial hardship or natural disaster.

6. Negative Narratives

According to Vantage Score, negative narratives are notations on your credit report that are derogatory. These cause the most harm and will keep your score from rising for longer time frames. Lenders consider such derogatory entries to be proof of debt that you mismanaged. It explains why the various credit scoring models count them as sufficient reason to allow significant and lasting reductions to your credit score.

You should avoid all of these 12 derogatory remarks if at all possible:

Foreclosure process started, foreclosure completed, Forfeiture of Deed in Lieu of Foreclosure, Redeemed Repossession, Repossession, Voluntary Repossession, Paid Charge Off, Account Charge Off, Account Included in Bankruptcy, Settlement Accepted on Account, Account Currently 30 (60, 90, or 180 days) past due, and Account assigned to external or internal collections agency[23].

7. Third Party Collections

As one of your accounts reaches the seriously delinquent point, the creditor may cut their losses by selling off the account to a third party collection agency. This could happen after they have made numerous attempts through their own internal collections department. After they have sold off your account to the third party, this in collection account can get reported on your credit report as a separate delinquent account.

This is part of the way that they create substantial negative effects on your credit scores.

Third party collections only appear on accounts that are unsecured (like personal loans or credit cards). Mortgages, car loans, and other secured loans show up as foreclosures or repossessions on your report. Repossessed car loans can also be sent out for third party collection. If your car is repossessed then sold at a steep discount at auction, then the recovered amount could be lower than your remaining balance, which would then be sent out for collections.

There are only two ways to have collections taken off of your credit report.

If the information reported is valid, it takes a full seven years from the first delinquency date for the information to drop off of your three reports. This delinquency date is the point from which your account first went delinquent (and you never again made it current).

If the information on collections is not accurate, you can always file disputes with the credit reporting bureau. This would result in the record either being removed or updated if the credit bureau rules that the dispute in your favor[24].

8. The Age of Your Credit History

The age of your credit history could be a positive or a negative influencer of your credit. Lenders consider this length of time to ascertain the chances of your repaying your loan or credit in a timely fashion. With a longer history, this demonstrates to them that you possess more experience exercising and managing credit successfully.

The theory goes that the longer amount of credit history you have, the more certain lenders are able to be in deciding the quantity of risk they are assuming in lending you money.

Opening or even closing an account can lower your credit score over the short term.

This is because it will reduce the average age of your credit accounts. If you close an existing credit account that has a longer credit history, this will likely cause a negative impact to your scores. This impact becomes more pronounced should you decide to close out a number of older accounts at a single time, per Vantage Score.

Opening new accounts waters down your length of credit history and can similarly cost you points, particularly if you open several new accounts in close proximity to one another[25].

9. Payday Loans

In general, Payday Loans do not negatively impact your credit score so long as you pay them back fully and in a timely manner. There could be an exception. Some lenders may regard Payday Loans as negative since they feel that customers of these loans are not as reliable a borrower as others. In such cases, having a Payday Loan on your personal credit history could harm your chances of getting approved for some loans.

It is important to keep in mind that you have more than a single credit score. The two major models of FICO and Vantage Score, as well as the three main credit reporting bureaus of Experian, Equifax, and TransUnion, all calculate scores differently using their own proprietary criteria.

The result is that Payday Loans can impact your various scores differently. Some lenders also do not distinguish between traditional loans and Payday Loans[26].

10. Unemployment

The personal information section of your credit report may list past or current employers. This is not promised to be a complete employment history or picture. Instead it is an employer list that was included in your past applications for credit that then reached the three main credit reporting bureaus (from your lenders).

This information is only obtained when you apply for a loan or credit, and not all lenders even report it. This explains why any employer list is not likely to be comprehensive. There are likely to be gaps shown in such an employment list (which depends on the last time you applied for credit).

The good news is that this will not create any impact on your credit history or score.

In fact, unemployment will never directly impact your credit scores. The reason is that your credit reports are not set up to prove if you are employed. Instead, they share information related to debt and credit. There could be an indirect effect of being unemployed revealed on your report if you can not make your timely monthly full debt payments because you are unemployed[27].

Additional Tips for Avoiding Declines in Your Credit Score

Besides these 10 negative credit impacting actions we have just gone through in some detail, there are some additional tips for avoiding hurting your personal credit score. These other eight practical ideas for maintaining your credit score include the following:

Never Ignore Possible Inaccuracies

Mistakes on credit reports happen all the time. Even if they are limited to only one percent of credit reports, this still amounts to over a million reports with potentially damaging misinformation. You can check your credit report for free (with no negative consequences) through a service like Credit Karma or Discover It or by contacting the three major reporting credit bureaus online (they will send you all three of your reports once per year at no charge) or by phone.

If you spot a mistake, no matter how small, make sure to file a dispute at your earliest convenience with the relevant credit reporting agency. It can take them up to a month to investigate and correct the error.

Paying Your Insurance Monthly

How you pay your car insurance premium does not directly impact your credit score. The way it can affect you is if you only pay it by the month (instead of quarterly or semi-annually). In monthly payment instances, the insurance provider will conduct a hard inquiry on your credit report since they are de facto extending you credit.

Each of these hard hits on your credit report has the potential to lower your score by several points, in particular if there are several of them at the same time. Avoid this by paying your car insurance premiums for a longer time period than only a month.

Beware of Transferring all of Your Credit Card Balances to a Single Card

This action may allow you to consolidate your debt and pay less interest, but it can cost you points in the credit utilization category (making up 30 percent of your total credit score). The reason is that the credit scoring algorithms check your balance on each card to determine per card credit utilization.

Anything over 30 percent utilization looks bad and costs you points, even if your average credit utilization is less than 30 percent.

Avoid Too Many Credit Requests

The component for new credit is 10 percent of your score. With each additional request for credit, this number of hard inquiries goes up. Several of them at once will cost you points in this category. Instead, make it a point to spread out your requests for new credit by several months if at all possible.

Withdrawing Cash on Credit Cards

The simple act of withdrawing a cash advance from your credit cards will not directly affect your personal credit score. The high costs surrounding these cash withdrawals will increase your monthly payment minimums.

If you become unable to keep up with the minimum payments in a timely manner, then this will badly impact your payment history component (counting for 35 percent of your score).

Your cash advance will also raise your credit utilization ratio.

If this drives the key number up above 30 percent, then you will lose points from the critical 30 percent component of credit utilization. Cash advances from credit cards may not appear as individual items on your report, but going over the key threshold in utilization will undoubtedly hurt your score every time[28].

Co-Signing on Credit Applications

It does not directly hurt your credit score to be a co-signer on someone else's loan. The way it can badly hurt you is if they do not meet the terms of their agreement by making on time payments. Even though this is their loan, your score will suffer in the payment history critical component (35 percent of score) if your co-signer falls behind or becomes delinquent on the loan.

The debt amount will also drive up your debt to income ratio, which lenders do consider in the approval process.

Beware of the Trap of Closing Too Many Credit Lines at a Time

It is tempting to close out credit cards that you simply do not use. The problem is that your credit score includes a 15 percent component for average age of accounts. With each account closed, you lower your credit's average age. This can cost you more points the more accounts you close at the same time. You should carefully consider closing existing accounts and spread them out if you do decide to go through with this[29].

Closing cards with 0 percent credit utilization can also harm your average credit utilization component of your score by driving it higher (a category that makes up 30 percent of your total score).

Closing Cards With Remaining Balances

Cancelling a card with a remaining balance will cause you to increase that card's credit utilization to over 100 percent (as the available credit will be $0 then). This would harm you in the crucial component of credit scores called credit utilization (making up 30 percent of your score).

A better way to do this would be to first pay off or transfer the balance (from the card you will close) to another card. Then the card will show a 0 percent utilization when you close it. Be careful about closing cards that you had for a long time as this will negatively impact your overall credit history length (the component making up 15 percent of your credit score[30]).

Now that you have a solid understanding of what makes up your credit score, positive ways to impact it, and negative actions to avoid harming it, we will move on to your understanding credit report in the next chapter to learn what your credit report really is all about.

Key Takeaways from this Chapter

Private and government liens and judgments no longer impact your credit reports and scores!

* * *

Short sales done properly will create a less negative effect on your personal credit score than an all out foreclosure will.

* * *

A late payment that is reported as 30 days or more past due could crash your credit score by up to 100 points.

* * *

The worst possible thing you can show in this category is over limit or maxed out card balances (amounting to 100 percent or higher utilization).

* * *

Opening or even closing an account can lower your credit score over the short term.

* * *

If you spot a mistake in your credit report, no matter how small, make sure to file a dispute at your earliest convenience with the relevant credit reporting agency.

* * *

Anything over 30 percent utilization looks bad and costs you points, even if your average credit utilization is less than 30 percent.

* * *

Your cash advance will also raise your credit utilization ratio.

CHAPTER

07

What Is A Credit Report?

Introduction

Understanding how the credit reporting bureaus compile your credit score (using either a FICO or Vantage Score model) is crucial. Yet you also need to understand the credit report that underlies the all important credit score. In this chapter, we will consider all of the various components of this personal credit report and how to effectively manage it to your best financial advantage.

It could make the difference between approval and disapproval on your next loan or credit card request.

Credit reports are statements that contain detailed information on your various credit activities and current credit status. This includes the present condition of your credit card accounts and your history of paying loans and bills.

The vast majority of consumers possess more than a single credit report. In fact you generally have three credit reports compiled by the major reporting bureaus Experian, Equifax, and TransUnion. These consumer reporting agencies (credit bureaus) gather and store all sorts of financial information on you that creditors submit to them. This comes from credit card companies, lenders, and other financial firms. Interestingly, creditors do not have to submit their data to all of the credit reporting bureaus or any of them if they so choose. Most send it to at least one of them though.

These reports are crucial because lenders employ them as a means to determine if they will extend credit or a loan to you and at what interest rate.

Lenders similarly use your credit reports to decide if you still meet their terms for an already existing credit account.

Still other companies could use your credit reports to decide whether or not to provide you with insurance (and at what premium), if they will rent an apartment or house to you, and at what deposit they will provide you with utilities, Internet, cable television, or cell phone plans. Even employers often will review your credit report in considering you for a potential job (in around half of all cases).

They can use your report as a deciding factor in whether or not to hire you over a competitor[31].

What Is Credit Monitoring?

Credit monitoring is a service that companies provide you. They will carefully watch changes in your patterns of borrowing behaviour to notify you if there may have been fraud in your name. They also monitor any changes to your status of creditworthiness.

Credit monitoring services track both credit scores and credit reports in this effort. You can use these services to protect yourself from identity theft, which has become a problem affecting over 48 million Americans in the last few years. Fraudsters can steal your personal identity or financial information in order to falsely take out credit in your name for their own gain. This could involve faking Medicare or Social Security claims or buying purchases online or in store illegally.

This kind of criminal activity is hard to pick up on until months after it has taken place, at which point your credit may have been severely wrecked. It can take months or even years to restore it after you have been a victim of identity theft fraud.

This is where credit monitoring services become so important. They will make you aware of any changes to your credit activity like the opening of new accounts or hard credit inquiries that signify a major purchase is happening (like a car). There are credit monitoring services that also provide comprehensive credit score tracking so that you are continuously aware of your credit quality. This enables you to make any necessary repairs or changes to your credit that would interfere with you taking out a mortgage, car loan, or new credit line.

Features and pricing for credit monitoring services range from one service to another. They can easily cost from $19.99 to $39.99 per month. There are financial institutions that will track your credit scores as a customer for free (on a limited basis). Paid services provide more complete scans of your Social Security, credit card, and bank account numbers.

According to the Balance, the best credit monitoring services in 2019 are Privacy Guard, Credit Karma, Identity Force, Identity Guard, Experian Identity Works, Ultimate 3B Credit Monitoring, and TransUnion Credit Monitoring. The only one of these that offers a free service for credit monitoring is Credit Karma.

I have this topic covered in detail in a separate chapter ‚Guarding Your Credit' toward the end of this book.

How Can You Monitor Your Credit Score?

Free credit monitoring from Credit Karma empowers you to keep an eye on your credit score. Credit Karma lets you check your credit score as often as you like, with no penalty resulting on your credit reports. Besides the ability to pull your score whenever you want, they will also let you pull your credit reports (though not full reports from all three bureaus) on demand.

Credit Karma even offers a free limited credit monitoring service that helps you to stay abreast of your credit. Whenever they observe any significant changes to your Equifax or TransUnion credit reports, they will dispatch an alert to you so that you can follow up on any suspicious activities before a fraudster does you great damage.

Getting started is a matter of signing up for a free Credit Karma account. The free credit score and monitoring they provide will enable you to catch either mistakes or identity theft signs in time to correct or address them before they cause you serious harm. Mistakes on your credit report prove to be more commonplace than you might expect.

These can cause you to pay higher interest rates or be rejected from credit applications for which you should be approved.

Meanwhile their credit monitoring will make it quicker and simpler to find suspicious activities on your report. Examples of these are new hard inquiries that someone makes on your report without asking you and newly opened accounts that you did not request. Monitoring your credit score and reports is a good financial habit that you should personally practice routinely or pay a service to do on your behalf.

How Can I see My Credit Score For Free?

There are two basic ways to see your credit score for free. Some credit card companies and banks provide a free credit score to you on your monthly statement. Examples of these providers are Capital One, Bank of America, and Barclays.

You can also create an account with one of the two best regarded free credit score companies Credit Karma or Discover It. Without having to link a credit card or sign up for a free trial, both companies will allow you to regularly check on your credit score and your credit report as many times as you like at no charge and without any hard inquiries on your credit report resulting from doing so.

Did you know that over *100 million Americans now have an account with Credit Karma and so keep an eye on their credit scores at no charge in this way.*

How To Read, Review, and Understand Your Credit Report

The easy part is obtaining your credit report for free from the three credit reporting bureaus (or from a service like Credit Karma or Discover It). Comprehending this information that they report can be challenging. There are several key sections on your credit reports.

We will look at each of them next along with terms they use that may not always be self explanatory. Remember that the credit reporting bureaus arrange their reports somewhat differently, meaning that the sections can be ordered differently with each report.

Personal Information

Included in your personal information section are your name(s), previous and current phone numbers and addresses, your birth date, Social Security number, and some previous (and possibly current) employers. Your name could be spelled differently in places thanks to any variations that you use on credit applications (married versus maiden names and with or without middle initials).

Do not be concerned about a telephone number or employer that may be missing. What you should watch for here in reviewing your credit report are any addresses that are not yours. This is especially troubling if you see accounts that are not yours alongside them. It could mean that someone has used your personal information to create false accounts for themselves in your name. The bills would be diverted to the false addresses so that you are not informed of the deception.

Accounts

In this crucial section are all of your accounts that are current (not defaulted on or sent out to collections). This remains the heart of your credit report. Every account will provide a critical summary underneath it in the beginning. This will include the following:

• Creditor's name and address, date opened, and account number

- Account Status – if the account is opened, closed, or transferred, and most importantly if you are current with your payments

- Account type – credit card, auto loan, student loan, etc.

- Your status – details whether you are a joint owner, an individual owner, or merely an authorized user on the particular account

- Total credit line or instalment loan original dollar amount – this includes all payment and balance information, such as the last date the creditor dispatched your account information update to the reporting bureaus. This will not reflect today's balance on your account. Even if you pay off your credit card full balance each month, the report could depict a balance if this activity was reported in the middle of your billing cycle

It is critical that you check carefully the payment history for any mistakes (like late payment notifications if you have always paid on time).

You need to be certain that all of your account limits are listed correctly, since this does impact your critical credit utilization ratio (which counts for 30 percent of your score).

Also if one of your accounts was closed, you should observe who closed the account and on what date for accuracy. Good standing closed accounts might remain indefinitely on your credit reports. If the creditor closed them because you did not meet your account terms as agreed, then these should drop off the credit report seven years after the first delinquency of the account.

Any Negative Information

This section of negative information details any accounts that were not paid according to the terms of agreement, public records of bankruptcies, and collections accounts.

This derogatory information remains on your report for a full seven years, besides Chapter 7 bankruptcies that hang around for 10 years.

If you have accounts listed in this section, you need to be certain that the negative information is fully accurate. If you see any incorrect collection or account listing information here then you need to file disputes for removal. Similarly if an item is listed after the seven year drop off period, you need to contact the credit reporting bureau right away.

Credit Report Inquiries

In this section, the bureaus detail all instances when a third party did a hard inquiry check on your credit. Each time that you ask for a credit limit increase or apply for new credit cards, loans, or even apartment/housing or utilities this will be noted.

These different entries are often separated out. Hard inquiries will be listed together for each time you allowed a possible creditor to investigate your file in the process of an application. Too many hard inquiries will lead to a drop in your credit scores that is temporary.

Soft inquiries do not impact your credit scores. They occur if you choose to check out your own credit report or score or if a promotional offer is sent out to you by a credit card company.

Each kind of inquiry will reveal the inquiring organization's name and address and the date of the relevant check. You should be certain that each hard inquiry was personally authorized by you so that it is not fraud. Also check to see that they have all fallen off from your report after two years have passed[32].

Do not be daunted by the appearance of complexity with your credit report. No one will show the care and concern to make sure entries are correct as passionately as you do. It is critical that you review your reports at the very least annually, if not multiple times a year.

What Makes the Three Credit Reporting Bureaus Different?

The very fact that there are three completely separate, important credit reporting bureaus (Experian, Equifax, and TransUnion) by definition means that they will be different. Credit bureaus are simply the firms that collect and store different kinds of credit information about you, your financial accounts, and your payment history.

They compile all of this information in order to build out your credit reports and determine the resulting credit scores. People mistakenly tend to throw the big three credit reporting bureaus into a single category, yet they compete against each other as independent entities for various creditors' business. Creditors come to them for your credit reports and scores to assist them in making responsible lending choices.

There are three main sources for the credit bureau data - these include:

1. Creditor-reported information to the bureaus – Banks, lenders, and creditors will report information on their customers and accounts to one or more of the big three bureaus. The bureaus call these creditors "data furnishers" in this capacity.

2. Information that the bureaus buy or gather themselves – Credit bureaus actually buy some data. LexisNexis sells public records as a consumer credit bureau itself, and the credit bureaus may purchase it to have the data when creating your credit report. This could include bankruptcy records, the only real public records information that counts on credit reports since the sweeping changes of 2017/2018.

3. Information the bureaus share between one another – The big three bureaus may be fierce competitors, but they do share information with each other sometimes. If you were to set a fraud alert or initiate a credit freeze with one of them, then they must share this alert with the other two bureaus.

You will see the differences between the three bureaus yourself if you compare your three credit reports. These can be important. Some creditors do not report to all three credit bureaus. Others may not report regularly to all three, or to any of them.

This is how you can end up with sometimes substantially different credit scores from varying credit reports. It results from the variations in data that each report contains[33].

Three Types of Consumer Credit And How You Can Access Them

There are actually three different categories of consumer credit today. These are revolving, instalment, and open. Each of them will affect your credit score in different ways. Possessing a variety of these credit types improves your credit score (in the 10 percent credit mix component). We will consider each of these three types and how you can access them next.

Revolving Credit

Proves to be among the most frequent kinds of credit accounts for consumers. This type of credit takes the form of a line of credit against which you can draw (or borrow) whenever you need it up to the maximum amount, or credit limit. This limit represents the maximum that you can put to use at any given point.

The most frequent types of revolving credit are credit card accounts and HELOCs, or Home Equity Lines of Credit. These generally require you to make consistent monthly payments and involve interest charges if you choose to carry a monthly balance (after the payment date).

Instalment Credit

Involves a preset, lump sum loan amount that comes with a regular and fixed schedule of repayment. There are many different loans that fall into this category. Some of them are mortgages, car loans, student loans, and personal loans. This is a second most common form of consumer credit.

Open Credit

The third type of credit is a rarer form called open credit. A great number of individuals do not have it on their personal credit reports at all. Open credit accounts are ones against which you are able to borrow up to a maximum cap. Yet they are different because you must pay them back in their entirety every month.

Open credit is most commonly connected to charge chards (not traditional credit cards). Many store accounts used to be charge cards, though most of these have converted to revolving credit nowadays. American Express is the greatest single remaining example of open credit these days. Any balances you charge on AMEX must be repaid by the statement due date each month[34].

What Is the Difference Between Hard and Soft Inquiries?

The primary difference between a hard and soft inquiry on your credit report is who is requesting it. When you check your own credit, it shows up as a soft inquiry.

Soft inquiries do not negatively impact your credit report in any way, even though the credit bureaus keep records of these soft hits just like they do hard hits.

Hard inquiries are another story. They represent an application for credit or a credit increase that you have initiated. One or more hard hits mean that you will probably be increasing your available credit or debt in the near future. Too many of these hard inquiries at one time together will cause you to lose points in the new credit component (representing 10 percent of your credit score).

You could see your score drop several points if you have too many of these at once. The easy solution is to spread out any new credit requests over time (at least from three to six months apart if you can manage it).

What Public Records Show Up On Your Credit Report?

In evidence that the credit reporting bureaus occasionally do something to provide relief to consumers, they enacted a sweeping change to the public records section of your credit reports in 2017 and 2018. They dropped all public records except for bankruptcies from all consumer credit reports over those two years. From then on, no more liens or judgments of any kind (court, private, or tax liens or judgments) will appear on your credit reports or influence your credit score.

Bankruptcies remain on your credit report for from seven to 10 years, depending on the type of bankruptcy that you file (Chapter 7 bankruptcies need 10 years to drop).

In the next chapter, we will look at understanding each of the items in your credit report in more detail. This can make a significant damage in the actions you take to positively (rather than negatively) influence your ultimate personal credit score.

Key Takeaways from this Chapter

Credit Karma offers a free limited credit monitoring service that helps you to stay abreast of your credit.

* * *

You need to be certain that all of your account limits are listed correctly, since this does impact your critical credit utilization ratio (which counts for 30 percent of your score).

* * *

Derogatory information remains on your report for a full seven years, besides Chapter 7 bankruptcies that hang around for 10 years.

* * *

Soft inquiries do not impact your credit scores. They occur if you choose to check out your own credit report or score or if a promotional offer is sent out to you by a credit card company.

* * *

One or more hard hits mean that you will probably be increasing your available credit or debt in the near future.

* * *

Spread out any new credit requests over time (at least from three to six months apart if you can manage it).

Understand What Is In Your Credit Report

Introduction

Now that you know what a credit report actually is and contains, you need to understand the various components of what is in your credit report and what this means for you personally. In this chapter we will look at the various moving parts of the credit report and why they matter in a more detailed breakdown.

Regardless of whether your credit score is good or less than optimal, you are better off knowing what is in your credit report. If your score is poor, then you can improve it by taking certain steps. If your score is good, then you are able to concentrate on maintaining this level.

Remember that it takes months and sometimes years to build up a solid credit history. By monitoring your report and score, you regain control over your credit. It also helps you to become more accountable for a credit score that is optimal.

This starts with ensuring that all of the information contained in your credit files is accurate.

If your score is lower than you think it should be, then this is likely a reflection of information contained in your credit report. There could be mistakes that are costing you significant points. Lower scores might be signs that your personal report has errors that you need to dispute with the big three credit bureaus as soon as possible.

Checking your credit report regularly means that you will not be blindsided by the results of new credit or loan applications. If you do not know where you stand, you could receive credit terms that are less positive than what you anticipated. Being aware of where your credit level is allows you to mentally and emotionally prepare yourself for any less than desirable outcomes.

By gaining real insight into actions that have harmed or helped your credit score, you will learn the ways that your financial choices are impacting your credit. You can witness how opening another credit card or paying down a balance will impact your score. After you have learned and personally seen how these choices determine your credit score, you will be better aware of what to do and especially what not to do before you apply for a significant loan application.

Checking your credit report also enables you to react to changes in your credit with more speed.

Routine checking of it will let you be aware of important changes that will impact your credit score much faster. Should your score fall, this will indicate that you need to go carefully through the information in your credit report files to see what created the damage. This will allow you to make changes that can help you to regain lost points from your credit score.

It will also help you to catch any potential fraud much quicker before severe damage can be done to your credit report and score[35].

Why Should You Use A Free Service Like Credit Karma?

The only way to see your credit report (more than once a year) for free is to sign up with one of the credit score services like Credit Karma or Discover It. If you go online or call the three major credit bureaus Equifax, Experian, and TransUnion, they will give you one free report per year. This is not nearly a frequent enough check of your personal financial health though.

With Credit Karma, you can check your credit scores and credit report as many times as you feel necessary at no charge. When you use one of these services, pulling your credit report only counts as a soft inquiry (meaning that it does not damage your credit score standing). Credit Karma also allows you to use their basic monitoring service for free. This will enable you to obtain weekly updates and critical periodic notifications if they find any changes to your credit score.

What Is In My Credit Report?

Your credit report is a file on you that includes your personal information, credit inquiries, credit accounts' history, and public records of bankruptcies. Your creditors and lenders report this information on to the three main credit bureaus of Experian, Equifax, and TransUnion. They then use it to compile your FICO score or Vantage Score so that other lenders will be able to learn all about how creditworthy you are.

While every one of these three credit reporting bureaus reports and formats your personal information in their own way, your reports will more or less have the identical groupings of information (if arranged differently). It is grouped in one of four categories. These categories include your identifying personal information, credit accounts, inquiries for credit, and public records (bankruptcies).

Personally Identifying Information

Under the category of personally identifying information you will find your name, date of birth, address, Social Security number, and at least some employment information. The credit reporting bureaus uses this to be able to identify you. None of this information feeds into your credit scores.

The updates in this information are derived from all credit applications you provide to lenders and creditors when you apply for any new credit.

It is crucial that you make sure the bureaus have correct identifying information on you. In particular if you see incorrect addresses that you do not recognize, this could be a troubling sign that a fraudster is targeting your individual identity for his own personal gain. You do not need to worry if all of your employers are not listed here, as none of this information has any bearing on your credit report or score.

Credit Accounts

Your various lenders and creditors will faithfully report your payment status on every account that you have opened with them. This will include the kind of account it is (whether mortgage, car loan, credit card, or other), the date of account opening, your loan amount or credit limit, your current account balance and history of payments, and whether or not you always make your payments in a timely fashion.

The two components of your credit score in this section include payment history (35 percent of your score) and credit utilization (30 percent). Between them, they amount to nearly two-thirds of your entire credit score calculation, making the information in this section the most critical for your credit score.

Be sure to keep your accounts in good standing and to keep an eye on this section for any mistakes or inaccuracies that can negatively impact your credit.

The two primary kinds of accounts listed here will be revolving accounts and instalment loans. The revolving accounts are your typical credit cards that allow you to use, pay down, and re-use your credit limits. The instalment loans are the ones that pay out a lump sum amount upfront (for a car purchase as an example) then you pay them down according to fixed, scheduled monthly payments.

This section will also provide key information on whether the accounts are open or closed. If the account is closed, it will give the information on who closed the account and the reason why. You should also check this information carefully on a regular basis too, as a mistaken reason for closing one of your accounts by your creditor could cost you points from your credit score.

Collection accounts are also listed in this section on your credit report. You want to avoid any of these if at all possible. When you fall behind on a credit or other revolving account by 180 days, the creditor will typically charge this account off and send it out for collections. The date of original delinquency and the collection company name will appear here along with the original debt amount.

This information remains on your credit reports for seven years and does great harm to your score. It can easily cost you 100 points so make every effort to keep past due accounts out of collection status.

Credit Inquiries

This third section of your credit report reveals your recent attempts to obtain credit to the bureaus. Any of your recent loan applications or credit card applications will show up here in the form of a hard inquiry, listing the name and date of the creditor who pulled your credit in support of an application. Because you have authorized the lender to receive a copy of your credit report, it will appear under credit inquiries.

This section maintains a full list of all companies who scrutinized your personal credit report over the past two years. It will not only show the hard inquiries, but also the soft inquiries (as when you receive pre-approved credit offers or check your own credit through a third party service like Credit Karma).

Lenders are only able to see the hard hits on your credit report. The soft hits are information only available to you personally. The good news is that these soft hits do not have any impact on your FICO or Vantage Scoring scores. You should be wary of too many hard hits at once though, as these depict you to be a higher credit risk to lenders and creditors. Too many hard inquiries will certainly cause your score to drop.

Public Records

In an unusual move back in 2017 and 2018, the credit bureaus worked together to provide some relief to consumers. They stopped recording all public records debts except for bankruptcies. Public and private judgments and liens (even tax liens) no longer show up in your public records section on your report, nor do any of the debts associated with these.

Bankruptcies still remain on your credit report from seven to 10 years from date of resolution[36].

Medical debts are part of the data that the credit bureaus have expunged back in 2017 and 2018. Medical bills on which you are behind will no longer show on your credit report nor impact your credit score any more. This is good news for many people, and it actually improved the scores of around six percent of consumers when it went into effect.

This change does not stop collectors and medical billing companies from trying to collect the debts you owe them however.

The Use of Section 809

Section 809 is an important part of the Fair Debt Collection Practices Act. It deals with the right to dispute debt collections by a consumer. You have the right to contact a collector regarding their attempts to collect a debt and request that they send you all of the important information concerning the debt.

The creditor must notify you in writing of all of the following:

- The total debt amount
- The creditor's name to whom you owe the debt
- A statement giving you 30 days from the receipt of the notice to dispute the debt's validity, otherwise the debt is reaffirmed by you.

- Another statement that declares if you write to dispute the debt, the collector will have to verify the judgment or debt against you and furnish you with a copy of this judgment or verification by mail

- A final statement that the collector will furnish you with the original creditor's name and address if it is different from the present creditor. They must do this within 30 days of receiving your request

Requesting information and verification of a debt (effectively disputing it) from the collector forces them to stop all efforts to collect on the debt up to the point that they get the verification of the debt or copy of the associated judgment.

They must then mail the name and address of the original creditor along with verification of the debt to you before they can resume any collection activities. If you do not dispute the debt's validity, you do not waive your rights to do this in the future.

Failing to do so will not be construed as admission of debt liability.

Important Sections of the Fair Credit Reporting Act

The Fair Credit Reporting Act is a 1970 era law passed to regulate the consumer credit bureaus and their collection and gathering of consumer credit information and access to their personal credit reports. Congress mandated it to deal with the accuracy, fairness, and privacy of personal information found in the credit reporting agencies' files.

This act covers a number of important elements, and it protects the rights of consumers in several key provisions. It limits the ways that these bureaus can gather and share information on individual consumers. Bureaus are limited to collecting information including an individual's past loans, bill paying history, and present debts. They are allowed to include information on employment, arrest records, previous and present addresses, and whether they have filed for bankruptcy too. It also provides rights to consumers such as the ability to freely access their own credit reports.

Finally, the FCRA creates a limit to who is permitted to see your credit report and in which circumstances. Lenders are allowed to request your report if you apply for a car loan, mortgage, or revolving credit. Insurance companies are permitted to review your report when you apply for insurance coverage. The government is also allowed to ask for it as part of a grand jury subpoena or a court order (or when you apply for government granted licenses).

The two primary government agencies tasked with enforcing and overseeing the provisions of this act are the CFPB Consumer Financial Protection Bureau and the FTC Federal Trade Commission. Besides this, a number of the individual states also maintain their own statutes that pertain to rules on credit reporting.

What Is Not On Your Credit Report?

According to FICO, your credit report does not gather or detail any information on your race, gender, national origin, religion, marital status, medical history, criminal record, political affiliation, or if you have ever obtained public assistance.

FICO does note that lenders are able to contemplate this information by requesting it in an application. They state that other types of credit scores may contain some of this information as well.

Key Takeaways from this Chapter

Checking your credit report enables you to react to changes in your credit with more speed.

* * *

With Credit Karma, you can check your credit scores and credit report as many times as you feel necessary at no charge.

* * *

Updates in your credit report are derived from all credit applications you provide to lenders and creditors when you apply for any new credit.

* * *

Collection accounts remains on your credit reports for seven years and does great harm to your score. It can easily cost you 100 points so make every effort to keep past due accounts out of collection status.

* * *

Bankruptcies still remain on your credit report from seven to 10 years from date of resolution.

* * *

Bureaus are limited to collecting information including an individual's past loans, bill paying history, and present debts.

* * *

Lenders are allowed to request your report if you apply for a car loan, mortgage, or revolving credit.

How To Use Credit Cards to Build Credit

Introduction

Now that you understand the components of your credit score, what is on your credit report, and why this matters, it is time to start putting it all together. In this chapter we look at the most effective way to build up your credit (or rebuild it).

This is by effectively using credit cards the smart way.

Two main factors affect the majority of your credit score. Whether or not you pay your bills on time (is worth 35 percent of your credit score) and the amount of your credit you are utilizing (is worth 30 percent). The two categories together comprise nearly two-thirds of your score all by themselves. It is not fast to establish a timely payment history.

This takes a good six months to a year of paying your bills by their due date, and the creditors reporting this to the big three credit bureaus Equifax, Experian, and TransUnion.

The second most important component of credit card utilization you can more quickly influence. If you are carrying larger balances, and can pay them down, this will give you points in the 30 percent category in as little as one to two months (how long it takes the credit reporting bureaus to get the update on your credit card balances).

By paying this down to under 30 percent utilization, you will quickly be rewarded. If you are able to pay it down to 10 percent or less, then you will receive maximum points in this critical category, and all without having to wait half a year or longer.

Remember this then: the fastest way to improve your poor credit score is to pay down your credit card account balances to less than 30 percent (or even 10 percent ideally).

Factors You Need To Consider When Choosing A Credit Card

It goes without saying that not all credit cards are created equally. You should only consider the best ones for your personal situation. Here are five factors to think about when you are looking for your first (or next) credit card:

Cost of Having the Card

Credit cards always come with fees, detailed in the fine print. The fee you need to be on the lookout for first is the annual fee for having the card. There is a trade off for cards that charge such a fee. They often provide a stronger rewards program which can offset the annual fee. Some cards will waive the first year's fee as a courtesy to new members.

Consider getting a card that does not charge a yearly fee. There are plenty of these from which you can pick.

Also watch out for foreign transaction fees, in particular if you travel a great deal. Credit card companies often assess a three percent fee for every dollar you spend in another currency. Once again, there are countless credit cards that do not charge such a fee, so think about whether or not this is important in your life.

APR or Annual Percentage Rate of the Card

This becomes important if you choose to carry a balance and not pay down the entire amount due by the monthly due date. In this case, interest will build on your carried balance. The credit card shows this APR as your interest rate, or what you will pay for the amount you carry.

Something to look out for is a low introductory APR.

These provide you with a pre-set period of lower interest rates (sometimes this is 0 percent). Some cards will also give you a balance transfer lower APR for moving a balance over from another card. This is a smart way to lower the total interest you will pay altogether if you are paying down a significant amount of credit card debt.

The key is that you always make the minimum payment due on time, otherwise the APR will typically reset to the much higher default rate. This is the highest interest rate possible to pay on this card.

It is recommended that you pay down the whole balance transfer before the expiration of the introductory period so that you do not pay substantially higher interest rates on the remainder of the balance.

Another thing to watch for is the grace period on your card. This is the days in between when you charge something and when the interest starts to be assessed. You should not settle for a card without a grace period. These typically last 20 to 25 days on most cards.

Go for as long a grace period as you can when selecting a credit card.

Rewards Programs

Among the greatest features of a good credit card is its (sometimes incredible) rewards program. For daily purchases you make, you earn points that you can use towards retail purchases, travel and trips, cash back, and other rewards. Obtaining the greatest amount of points requires that you select a credit card that rewards you most generously where you spend the most money, such as grocery stores, gas stations, online retailers, and specialty shops.

The key is not to overspend what you intend so that your rewards program does not end up costing you dearly.

Credit Limit

You want a card that offers a high enough credit limit to have sufficient flexibility without being tempted to get into a runaway debt situation that you can not manage. College students are best suited with lower limit choices as they learn to responsibly use credit. After college, it helps to have a larger limit sufficient for your bigger monthly expenses.

A higher limit is also good in keeping your credit utilization ratio down.

This makes up 30 percent of your credit score, with the algorithms looking for less than 30 percent total utilization on each card and for your monthly average of all cards.

Customer Service

You should anticipate having to speak with your credit card company customer service department several times per year. This could be as simple as understanding some charges you made or as desperate as dealing with fraud on your card.

You need to talk with someone who is helpful, understanding, and competent to address your problems fast. If you notice the prospective credit cards have difficult to navigate web pages or keep you on hold on the phone for a long time when you call them, then you should be warned to expect more of the same once you are an existing customer.

You do not need to settle for poor customer service where your finances are concerned[37].

10 Myths Keeping You From A Good Credit Score

1. It Needs a Lot of Time for Your Credit Score To Become Bad

While it takes sometimes years to build up a good credit score, you can destroy it in a matter of months. Once your accounts are six months overdue, the creditor will simply charge them off. This is among the most damaging things that can afflict your personal credit score.

It only needs a few accounts charged off to collections for you to entirely ruin your credit score.

2. Checking Out Your Credit Will Harm Your Score

Actually you are able to pull your own credit report and score as often as you like without damaging it a bit. The key is to use the third party credit scoring services like Credit Karma or Discover It rather than creditors to view it. You are the only one who will see the resulting soft hits on your credit report from you checking it out.

3. Bad Credit Scores Hang Around Forever

Bad credit scores only remain terrible for all time if you continuously harm your credit score by maxing out credit cards, paying balances late, and allowing your accounts to be sent out for collections. If you begin to effectively and properly manage your own credit, your personal score will get better with time. How much time depends on how badly you damaged it in the first place.

4. You Must Earn A Lot of Money to Attain A Good Credit Score

The amount of money you earn only indirectly impacts your credit score. Income is not a determinant in your score at all. Your ability to pay your bills is what the algorithms are concerned about. Regardless of the amount of money you possess, paying your bills on time is critical as the smartest way you can positively impact your credit score (and it counts for 35 percent too).

5. Every Person Only Has One Credit Score

You will always have a few credit scores thanks to the varying credit score models in existence. The two models of FICO and Vantage Scoring draw on three different major credit bureaus for their data, meaning that you have at least six main credit scores altogether. Generally these will not vary by more than a few points from one another.

6. Prepaid and Debit Card Use Will Build Up Your Credit Score

If you think that gaining a debit card or prepaid credit card will boost your credit score, you are mistaken. Neither of these types of cards have a credit feature to them. Your card history with either type does not factor into your credit score or appear on your credit report. Try getting a secured credit card instead. Otherwise, the main products you want to build up your credit are loans, credit cards, and store charge cards. Having more of these varieties will help you in the credit mix category that makes up 10 percent of your FICO score.

7. Closing Credit Cards Will Boost Your Score

Actually you are more likely to do harm to your credit score than to improve it when you close out credit cards. If you close a card that still has a balance, this is especially the case. It is generally better to leave open accounts with good payment histories. This will help you keep your credit utilization down to under 30 percent (for 30 percent of your score). Open timely paid accounts show a positive payment history too (for 35 percent).

8. Having Money In Your Bank Account Improves Your Credit Score

Credit scores do not at all consider bank account balances (or assets of any kind). It is likely that good credit history corresponds to having savings, but this is unproven. There are many professionals with a great deal of money who have poor credit scores for not paying off their bills or making their payments on time every month. In today's world, a higher credit score is likely better for you financially than saved money in the bank, if you have to choose between the two.

9. Paying Off A Collection Account Will Stop It From Hurting Your Credit Score

Repaying collection accounts will improve your credit score over the longer term, but it will not provide you with an instant boost when you pay off a collection. Collection accounts remain on your credit report for seven years regardless of whether you pay them off or not. This will harm your credit score until it drops off finally.

Collections less than $100 do not have much impact if the lender is using one of the newer credit scoring models that disregards such low collection account amounts. You are better off paying down a balance on an account in good standing (which will immediately improve your credit utilization component) than paying off a collection account.

10. It Needs Seven Years to Improve Poor Credit Scores

The majority of negative information that finds its way on to your credit report lasts for seven years. The good news is that as this derogatory information gets older, it has a smaller impact on your credit score. By making on time payments and maintaining a manageable level of debt (to under 30 percent of your credit utilization), you can significantly improve your personal credit score long before the derogatory remarks drop off your credit report[38].

There Is No One Size Fits All Credit Card

As with most things in life, there is no such a thing as a one size fits all credit card. Credit cards were designed with many different individuals in mind. Here are nine different types of credit cards, some of which will fit your situation better than others do.

Unsecured Credit Cards

These are the most typical kinds of credit cards today. They are generally intended for individuals who have a range of from fair to excellent credit

Secured Credit Cards

These cards usually make you pay a security deposit in cash. It usually equates to all or half of the credit card limit. These cards are intended for those individuals who either lack credit or need to work on rebuilding their credit

Balance Transfer Credit Cards

Such cards allow you to transfer credit card balances from other credit cards to the new one in an effort to save on interest costs. Usually such new cards come with an introductory rate of 0 percent APR for a certain amount of time

Travel Rewards Credit Cards

This type of card gives you either points or miles which you can later redeem for purchases related to travel like hotels and airfares

Cash Back Rewards Credit Cards

Such credit cards give you a pre-set percentage in cash back on all eligible purchases

Gas Rewards Credit Cards

This card type rewards you with cash back when you use it at gas station pumps

Zero Percent Intro APR Credit Card

Such cards permit you an extended interest free grace period for upfront balance transfers and purchases

Student Credit Cards

Intended to be starter credit cards that can help you to establish or rebuild your credit, they usually start with smaller credit lines

Retail Cards

A card that is valid at one set retailer, it provides you with point rewards for goods or services that you purchase at that retailer

With all of these credit cards, it is critical that you discipline yourself and remember that credit is not a cash substitute. Anything that you charge you need to be able to repay. Otherwise you will fall into a seemingly never ending debt trap.

Remember that some debts are better than others too. Debts that you have the money already in the bank to pay off are good ones that help you to build your credit by paying them on time.

Debts for which you can not afford the purchase you are making are bad ones[39].

The Top 10 Strategies to Build Good Credit

There are some strategies to building up good credit that you should follow to maximize your efforts. We look at the top ten of these next.

1. Borrow Only What You Can Afford to Pay For

Remember that credit cards are not intended to help you finance things you can not afford. The most optimal way to build up solid credit is to only charge what you can comfortably afford. This will show potential creditors and lenders that you are a responsible user of credit and debt. It will also make it easier to obtain additionally needed credit in the future.

Avoiding excessive debt is critical. Your credit score is really a reflection of your success with only borrowing what you can readily repay.

2. Remember to Use a Small Part of Your Total Available Credit

Credit algorithms consider maxing out your credit cards to be the height of irresponsibility. Lenders are well aware that those who borrow to their maximum limits struggle to repay what they have originally borrowed. Exceeding 30 percent of your available credit, even if you pay it off on the due date every month, will cost you points in the critical credit utilization category comprising 30 percent of your score.

3. Start with a Single Credit Card

It can be a mistake to gather an assortment of credit cards in your first few years of having credit. The more you possess, the greater the temptation is to run them up and fall behind on payments and balances. By starting with only a single credit card, you will gain more points in the new credit category (that makes up 10 percent of your score) as you will not suffer too many hard inquiries on your credit report.

Too many new cards also reduce your average credit age, which makes up another 15 percent of your score.

4. Pay Off Your Full Credit Card Balance Every Month

In the theme of only charging what you can actually afford, pay off your entire credit card balance each month. This gives you major points in the 35 percent most important category of payment history and the 30 percent category for credit card utilization. Lenders and creditors love to see this, and your credit score reflects that bias.

Two-thirds of your credit score is based on this kind of responsible use of your credit!

5. Make Sure All of Your Payments Are on Time

Any bill that you do not pay on time has a habit of finding its way on to your credit report. Pay all of them on time and you will not become delinquent or even worse sent out to collections by a third party. Building a good credit score is a function of avoiding these negative accounts.

It can cost you 100 points from your credit score for every debt collection account that you have!

6. Balances Should Only be Carried the Smart Way

It is not always bad to carry a credit card balance if you do it smartly. Pay a larger amount than the minimum monthly payment to get these down as fast as possible.

Be sure to never be late with your credit card balances.

If you do carry debt, make sure it is less than the 30 percent magic number that the credit bureaus want to see (so you get full credit in the 30 percent credit utilization category).

7. Let Your Accounts Age

Longer time with credit is considered better for your personal score. Always keep oldest accounts open, as they boost your average credit age and build your credit profile up quickest. Closed accounts do not drop immediately off of your profile, but will fall off after two years generally. Credit age accounts for 15 percent of your score[40].

8. Try for a Mix of Credit Types to Improve Your Score

Rather than having two credit cards, try to get a second card as a charge card from a store or AMEX. Having variety in your credit like loans and charge cards adds to your credit mix category of 10 percent.

9. Do Not Apply for Too Many Credit Cards or Loans at Once

Your score has a 10 percent component for new credit inquiries. You can get full points in this category by not applying for too many credit cards or loans within a six month period. Spread out your credit requests and avoid those hard inquiries on your credit report as much as possible. These should be easy points to get.

10. Do Not be Afraid to Ask a Co-Signer to Help You Build Credit

If you are having trouble getting approved for good credit card offers or loans, get a co-signer. You then get the benefit of building your credit with timely payments off of their established credit history. This is a fast way to improve your credit score if you do not overextend this credit and you make the payments on time faithfully.

Striving for Excellent Credit - Attain An Over 700 Credit Score

According to The Motley Fool and FICO, around 23 percent of American consumers today possess a credit score of 800 or higher (out of a total 850 maximum possible points). This should encourage you to reach for a credit score of at least 700, something you can easily hope to achieve[41].

The bad news is that FICO jealously guards the particulars of its formula (though it reveals the five categories and their percentage components). This makes it impossible to tell you precisely what you need for perfect credit scores.

We do know the credit choices that the consumers in the highest credit ranges make though. These actions include the following:

- Average revolving credit lines are around 12 years old – with their first revolving credit card account opened up over 25 years ago. Length of credit history counts for 15 percent of total score with FICO.

- They have not experienced hard inquiries on their credit report in nine months.

- An impressive 95 percent of these high credit consumers (over 800 score) suffer from no delinquent credit accounts on their personal credit report.

- Their typically 10 active revolving credit accounts combined contain an average carried balance of $1,446.

- This under $1,450 in carried debt consumes a mere four percent of the high credit score consumers' available credit limit. The average 800 plus score holders do not apply over 10 percent of any of their revolving credit accounts.

Such behaviour will help you score well over 700 personally. If you combine all of these credit characteristics in your lifestyle effectively, then you may even top 800 points.

Three Factors That Influence the Timeframe to Improve Your Credit Score

The time frame to improve your credit score is based on your ability to improve in the three highest counting credit score categories. According to FICO, these are your timely payment history (for 35 percent), your credit utilization ratio (for 30 percent), and your length of credit history (for 15 percent).

Your payment history is the most important category.

It takes up to six months to demonstrate a timely payment history that is up to date with the big three credit reporting bureaus of Experian, Equifax, and TransUnion.

Credit Utilization is a quicker time component. This is updated every month. In theory, if you paid down your balances in June to less than 30 percent, then by July or at the latest August your credit report and score would reflect the lower credit utilization ratio and give you the increased points in this second most important category.

Length of credit history takes time to build up. In this category they are looking at your oldest account as well as the average age of all your revolving accounts. By not opening new credit cards, you can help your established credit to age faster. You can always open new credit, but if you do this then try not to make too many applications at one time.

These hurt you in two ways. More new accounts water down your length of credit history category. They also create multiple hard inquiries on your report, hurting your new credit component (comprising 10 percent of your score).

Your Credit Card Purchases Do Matter

It matters significantly how much you rack up each month in credit card spending. Even if you pay it off by the due date, your creditor will report your balance for the month to the three credit reporting bureaus.

This will worsen your credit utilization ratio, incorporating a critical 30 percent of your credit score.

If you must make routine large purchases with your credit cards, try paying an extra payment ahead of the due date each month to keep the balances low and manageable looking to the credit scoring algorithms.

The Truth About Credit Card Limits

The truth about credit limits is that your creditors never intended for you to use your entire credit card limit. Think of these amounts as a test of your responsibility and self control. The scoring algorithms want to observe how well you can handle this tantalizing credit line. They like to see you use less than 30 percent of your available credit (and even better less than 10 percent).

Certainly this is a guideline and not a hard and fast rule. One thing is certain with this critical component of your credit scoring model: the lower your total credit utilization proves to be, the better your score will be.

Under the Vantage Scoring model (and per Experian), exceeding the 30 percent credit utilization level will cost you significantly in points. Remember that those consumers who possess a FICO score of 800 are only using an average of seven percent of their total available credit[42].

The Best Strategies to Repay Your Debt

The best credit card balances to pay down first are those with the highest interest rates. By reducing the monthly balance that you carry, it will lower the amount of interest that is tacked on to your balance every month. This will save you interest expense (real money over time) and reduce the amount of time you need to pay off your overall bills.

You may find yourself in a position of too much debt and not have a clue as to how to efficiently pay it down. According to Business Insider, there are give good strategies that you can use effectively to help you escape from too much debt.

This starts with asking your creditor for a lower interest rate. If you have paid your bills on time for years, they may just agree.

A lower interest rate will decrease the additional charges that are being added to your account balance each month. If you combine your request for a lower interest rate with an offer to make a larger lump sum payment on the balance while talking with them, it might convince them to help you.

Secondly, you should also try to make double your minimum monthly due payment. This will dramatically reduce your balance and the length of time you need to pay it down. Third, experts recommend that you go after the most expensive interest rate debt first. Anything that you can pay over the monthly minimums due will always help reduce interest costs and time frame to repay your balances.

Avoid making only minimum payments as much as you possibly can.

You have two other options to reduce interest rates on high credit card balances. You could try to open a balance transfer card and move the balance over to a zero percent promotional offer. You might also apply at a bank or online for a personal loan and pay down the highest interest rate balances on your credit cards. Using these strategies can cut your repayment time frames down on high APR debt by as much as half[43].

Additional Credit Card Considerations

Joint accounts are only as good as the least disciplined person on the account. Whether or not your joint account holder makes minimum payments or pays off their charges, you will ultimately also be responsible for these in any event. Your credit score will be impacted by their not making timely payments, so be very careful of the person you open a joint account with on a credit card.

Remember that there is no such a thing as a joint credit score, only two credit scores that are equally impacted by the decisions that the joint account holders make.

You want to be extremely careful about closing existing accounts. This hurts you in the credit age category (counting for 15 percent) as it reduces your average credit card account age. It will also generally increase your credit utilization ratio. If it jumps this number to over 30 percent, you will lose significant points in this second most important scoring category (that counts for 30 percent).

In general, you should only close an account if the annual fees are so high that you can not justify keeping it open. It is a better idea to call and discuss your concerns with the creditor.

They may be wiling to waive the annual fees for a year to keep you as a customer, in particular if you are regularly using the card or carrying a balance on it.

If you can manage to qualify for a no annual fee credit card, this is always a great benefit. It allows you to use the creditor's money every month for the length of the grace period (20 to 25) days at no cost to you. If you do not carry a balance each month, then the cost of the credit to you is effectively zero.

The trade off to a no annual fee credit card is often that they will not usually offer a rewards program.

For many people this is an unacceptable trade off. These credit cards rewards and points programs have turned out to be more popular than ever before. If you use them to attain the maximum cash back or travel rewards possible, it can easily exceed the annual fee for having the card and its lucrative rewards program. Some of these cards like the Chase Sapphire Rewards give you even $700 in free travel if you harness the opening charging bonus to its fullest extent.

Which Is More Appropriate For You: A Personal or Business Credit Card?

There are some key differences between the two types to consider. Business credit cards will affect both personal and business credit profiles. The lines between the two tend to blur. You will likely be required to sign a personal guarantee for any small business cards. This means that if your business misses any payments, then you will still be liable to make them personally.

A number of issuers will consider your personal credit score heavily in determining whether to extend credit to your business and how much to give you. They will report it to your business credit profile, but this may also spill over to your personal credit report.

American Express and Capital One proactively report this business credit activity to both business and consumer credit bureaus. Chase and others only report to the commercial credit bureaus but will make a special report to consumer ones if you fall behind on your payments.

One distinct advantage to business credit cards is that the credit limits tend to be higher. This is helpful if you actively are making expensive purchases. A higher limit will make it easier to keep that all important credit utilization ratio down, especially if you are making larger purchases every month.

There are also different rewards with business credit cards. These bonuses often apply to WiFi costs, phone bills, or office supplies. This will be less helpful to sole proprietors who use these items more sparingly. In many cases, you are better off with a standard rewards program which permits you to gain bonuses for all purchases, or with just getting a personal credit card and its accompanying rewards program.

How To Manage A Balance Transfer on Credit Cards

First you gather up your highest interest rate credit card balances. Get the statements so that you have all of the information necessary to transfer them to your new zero percent balance transfer offer. Next you will need to have your balance transfer offer ready to hand. They may have you send out checks included in the offer to your existing creditors to transfer the balances. More and more these days it is all handled online by logging on to the offering card's site and filling in the appropriate information to transfer the balances over electronically.

It is important to keep in mind the end of your promotional period on this zero percent interest rate transfer. You want to pay it off before it defaults back to the higher interest rate.

You can take the number of months in the promotional period and divide this into the total amount of debt you have transferred to come up with your required monthly payment to liquidate all of the transferred debt in time.

For example, if you are transferring $3,000 to a zero percent balance transfer offer that is good for 24 months, you would divide the $3k by 24 to come up with a necessary monthly payment amount of $125. By making this payment faithfully every month, you would have repaid the entire transferred balances amount in time to avoid any interest charges for carrying the debt.

Beware the Risk of A Department Store Card

There are really two principal risks in a department store charge card. One is that you may feel like the credit limit is a type of magic money, happily charging items that you can not really afford and would not buy in the first place if you instead paid with cash. The second danger arrives with the bill. You can easily get in over your head so that you can not pay the full bill when it arrives after the grace period is over.

Then you will either default on the card terms to repay the full amount each month, or if your card allows for you to carry a balance, you will pay the substantial APR interest rate charges each month until you finally pay down the balance.

The key discipline you need with these charge cards is to only buy what you can comfortably afford to pay off every month and nothing more.

Key Takeaways from this Chapter

The fastest way to improve your poor credit score is to pay down your credit card account balances to less than 30 percent (or even 10 percent ideally).

* * *

Consider getting a card that does not charge a yearly fee. There are plenty of these from which you can pick.

* * *

Go for as long a grace period as you can when selecting a credit card.

* * *

A higher limit is good in keeping your credit utilization ratio down.

* * *

It only needs a few accounts charged off to collections for you to entirely ruin your credit score.

* * *

It is generally better to leave open accounts with good payment histories.

* * *

Avoiding excessive debt is critical. Your credit score is really a reflection of your success with only borrowing what you can readily repay.

* * *

Too many new cards also reduce your average credit age, which makes up another 15 percent of your score.

* * *

It can cost you 100 points from your credit score for every debt collection account that you have!

* * *

Be sure to never be late with your credit card balances.

* * *

Your payment history is the most important category.

* * *

If you have too much debt, ask your creditor for a lower interest rate. If you have paid your bills on time for years, they may just agree.

* * *

Avoid making only minimum payments as much as you possibly can.

* * *

Keep in mind the end of your promotional period on this zero percent interest rate transfer. You want to pay it off before it defaults back to the higher interest rate.

Best Credit Practices Based on Your Age and Profession

There is no one size fits all credit card. Depending on your age and profession you will find certain credit cards more advantageous for your specific needs. In this chapter, we will look at the best credit cards for where you are in your own life.

Best Credit Cards for Starters

As a first time credit card user, the deck is stacked against you. These cards help you to overcome these sometimes seemingly insurmountable odds and establish a credit history. Such cards maintain minimal (if any) credit requirements and allow you to routinely access your credit score for free. They also deliver low costs and APR as well as rewards programs. Unlike most credit cards out there, these do not expect a credit history for you to qualify.

Best All Around Starter Card

Wells Fargo Cash Back College is the best all around credit card starter. It is oriented to students, but lets anyone without a credit history enjoy the exciting features of credit, like no annual fees, a zero percent intro APR on balance transfers and initial purchases, and a rewards program as well.

Best Secured Card for Starters

Discover It Secured is the best secured card for starters. With this card, you will be expected to make a deposit against your credit card limit. As a first time secured card goes, it provides you with a good rewards program and a low deposit amount. After you have successfully made eight months of timely payments to the account, Discover will contemplate returning your deposit back to you. This could be your best way to go for a first time credit card.

Best No Major Fees Starter Card

Petal Credit Card is famous for not charging any significant fees of any kind. You do not encounter any foreign currency transaction fees, late payment fees, or even annual fees with Petal. This is the card for you who want to build up your credit while spending nothing for the privilege.

Best Low APR Credit Card for Starters

SKYPASS Visa Secured Card is your best bet for a low APR card for starters. It is the only secured credit card that permits you to earn miles for airlines, and it also comes with a comparatively lower APR for starters. It may seem to you that 17.99 percent interest is not so low, but this is actually competitive compared to most starter credit cards today. Make sure to pay off your monthly balances each month, and you will avoid these costly fees[44].

Best Credit Building Cards for Teens, Students, and Young Adults

Next we look at credit cards to help teens, students, and young adults to build up good credit from scratch. The best starter cards in these categories enable you to establish credit without having to pay dearly in fees or to give up all of your rewards benefits. Here we look at four of the top recommended cards in this category from Credit Karma.

Best Rewards Program for College Students

Journey Student Rewards by Capital One offers the best rewards program for college students. You get cash back for every purchase. They also give you additional advantages when you engage in good credit behaviour. With no annual fee, the company makes money on the back end. If you carry a balance, it will cost you a dear 26.99 percent APR in interest. Pay your full balance each month and you can avoid this entirely.

Best Secured Credit Card for Students and Teens

For the best secured card for teens and students, Credit Karma suggests the Discover It Secured Credit Card. Besides no annual fee, you get a rewards program and the opportunity to retrieve your deposit after eight months of timely payment history. They also provide you with an impressive two percent in cash back on purchases at restaurants and gas stations on your first $1,000 in combined category purchases for every quarter (and one percent thereafter). Discover goes all in by matching your first year's cash back as well.

Best Rewards Card for Good Credit Graduates

Chase Freedom hits a home run with this best rewards card for those college grads with good credit. They offer a generous sign up bonus and the chance to learn the best ways to optimize your rewards programs. You start with a $150 bonus after spending only $500 on purchases in the first three months of the account.

Best Card for Limited Credit College Grads

Capital One offers its <u>QuicksilverOne Cash Rewards Credit Card</u> as a way for college grads with limited credit to improve their credit scores to the from good to excellent range. You earn terrific rewards as you use this card too. Established for people who only possess average credit, it works great if your credit history is limited and assuming that you have no recent account defaults.

It is no small thing to find a fair credit score card that provides a fantastic rewards program. QuicksilverOne gives you solid 1.5 percent cash back for each purchase you charge. They also promise a review for a credit line increase after making timely payments in your first five months.

Best International Student Credit Card

The vast majority of credit card issuers in America require that you possess a Social Security number in order to apply for their card. The <u>Deserve Edu Mastercard</u> is a notable exception for international students. The card comes with nice reward perks too. Approved applicants get as much as $59 in Amazon Prime Student subscription reimbursements. You can also count on their full one percent cash back on every purchase you charge with this credit card[45].

Best Credit Building Cards for Families

If you find yourself with a new and growing family, it is a good bet that you will need credit cards that grow into this role alongside your newfound expenses and responsibilities. Such credit cards understand your new family's needs and provide significant rewards for purchases like school supplies, diapers, and family getaways. We look at five of the most family friendly credit cards next, as recommended by Credit Karma.

Best Family Card for Cash Back

Parents would struggle to outperform the Blue Cash Preferred Card by American Express. It offers six percent cash back on all American supermarket purchases. You get this incredible cash back rate for your first $6,000 in annual purchases and then a one percent base rate on everything after.

Best Credit Card for New Parents

The Citi Double Cash Card is a lifesaver for new parents. It eliminates the need for tracking cash back expenditures and categories as well as having to activate cash back programs. This flat rate cash back card is no frills and no nonsense. Besides this, it provides you with an impressive two percent cash back on all purchases, significantly better than most competitors' 1.5 percent cash back rate.

Best Credit Card for Family Travel

Chase Sapphire Reserve is a great card for families who travel. It does flexibility extraordinarily well. The card starts with a yearly $300 travel credit for any qualifying travel purchases you charge. You also receive three points for each one dollar you spend in the restaurant and travel categories in the U.S. and abroad. All other category purchases earn you one for one rewards points for every dollar you spend.

Best Credit Card for College Savings

Upromise is the name brand in the college bound savings plans. Its Upromise MasterCard makes it easy to save for the future, with 1.25 percent in cash back for each dollar spent on any purchases. If you link up your Upromise Program account to a 529 college savings plan that is eligible, you also receive a 15 percent bonus on all earned cash back. This helps you to allocate a more serious amount of money to your children's college savings. Thanks to this linking bonus, you are looking at roughly 1.44 percent cash back on all purchases you make.

Best Credit Card for Online Shopping

Online shopping has its own best credit card category these days. Amazon Prime Rewards Visa Signature Card is just what the doctor ordered if you buy those constantly needed supplies for your growing children from the online retailing giant.

All Amazon Prime members who are cardholders automatically receive an impressive five percent in cash back on each one dollar you spend with the Prime Rewards Visa Signature Card at either Amazon.com or Whole Foods Market. Every dollar spent on gas stations, drug stores, and restaurants earns you two percent cash back. All other purchases get one percent cash back as a base rate. It adds up pretty fast[46].

Best Credit Building Cards for Lower Income Earners

In today's increasingly digital world, credit cards are now a necessity. The good news is that they do not have to be a costly one. If you suffer from fair or bad credit, you may just be starting your credit history or rebuilding it after having made some credit mistakes.

Low income earners find obtaining good credit cards especially challenging, but it does not have to be. Fair credit applicants can select between no annual fee cards or rewards cards with an annual fee. We look at the best credit cards for low income earners with fair and bad credit next.

Best "Fair" Credit Cards

The <u>Capital One Platinum Credit Card</u> offers a perk to low income earners in the form of no annual fee. After you make your first five timely monthly payments, they may give you a higher credit line too. You get full fraud coverage and online banking access as well.

Meanwhile, the <u>Credit One Bank Platinum Visa</u> offers you no annual fee, a comparatively competitive APR, and a one percent cash back rewards program for all purchases. You also get access to your Experian bureau credit score online for free each month, and you can even select your own payment due date.

Best "Bad" Credit Cards

The <u>Capital One Secured MasterCard</u> offers low income earners with bad credit a no annual fee credit card with all of its advantages to building up your credit. Capital One pledges to report your history to all three of the major consumer credit bureaus. You make a cash deposit of $49, $99, or $200 and receive a starter credit line of $200. Once you have made your first five monthly payments in a timely fashion, you will receive a higher credit limit too.

Another one to consider is the <u>Milestone MasterCard</u> that allows you to pre-qualify without having to suffer a hard credit inquiry on your credit report. They provide fraud protection and mobile account access to your account. This is a no frills card intended for people recovering from past credit mistakes, and it reports payment history to all three credit reporting bureaus[47].

Best Credit Building Cards for High Rollers

High rollers are at that eviable stage in life where they enjoy being handsomely rewarded for their business. This is where the premium credit cards come in with their larger than life rewards. Higher rewards rates, travel credits, and richer redemption choices are several of the advantages that premium card holders can look forward to receiving.

Obviously not just anyone will qualify for these types of high end credit cards. They are designed and targeted towards consumers who boast from good to fantastic credit. There is a considerable cost for these cards too. Their annual fees start at a hefty $250 and run to $450 and higher. It makes it critical to be sure that you can gain more value than the costs you pay when you apply for these premium credit cards. We look at the top five of them next.

Best All Around Premium Card

<u>Chase Sapphire Reserve</u> has been impressing high rollers for years. Besides the huge sign up bonuses (that amount to $750 in travel credits), the ongoing rewards are extensive. Best of all, as a card holder you have a great

amount of flexibility in redeeming such rewards, offering a wide selection of hotel chains and airlines as redemption partners.

Best Luxury Travel Perks

The Platinum Card from American Express defines luxury travel. Their welcome offer is generous, the redemptions choices are rich, and rewards rates are high. You get perks such as access to airport lounges and no cost hotel benefits that would cost hundreds of dollars. Every feature of the Platinum Card from American Express oozes luxury.

Best Premium Airline Card

Citi AAdvantage Executive World Elite card is ideal for you who travel frequently with American Airlines. The perks include such things as access to the Admirals Club airport lounge, free checked bags for yourself and as many as eight travelling companions, and zero foreign currency transaction fees. This checked bag credit could save you nearly $500 if you travel with the eight maximum companions.

Best Premium Dining Card

The American Express Gold Card wins in the category of Best Premium Dining Card. It boasts excellent travel and rich dining rewards along with valuable credits. Thanks to this card, the expenses of indulging in luxurious dining are a little less costly.

Best Business Travel Card

If you are looking for the best in class business travel card, look no further than the American Express Business Platinum Card. Its perks include access to airport lounges, high rewards, credits for airline costs, and status with their partner hotels. All of these benefits ensure that the AMEX Business Platinum card is ideal for business travellers[48].

Best Credit Building Cards for Business

Any individual who has a business is able to apply for one of these business cards. You do not have to be officially incorporated or boast employees to be counted as an owner of a business. The top credit cards for small business owners have to offer the most value possible. Maximizing profits while reducing costs is a top set of priorities for small business owners. Here we will look at the best business cards for larger purchases, travel and cash back rewards, and for building your credit up.

Best Overall Credit Card

The Ink Business Unlimited credit card is a leader with its no annual fees, cash back rewards, and even low initial purchase APRs. Its sign up bonus is an incredible $500 after spending at least $3,000 over the first three months. You also benefit from a 12 month long zero percent APR on all purchases and balance transfers, so long as you pay your monthly bill on time throughout the duration of the promotional period.

Best Credit Card for Travel Rewards

The ultimate credit card to have in your wallet for travel rewards proves to be the Citi Business AAdvantage Platinum Select World MasterCard. These miles reward get you 2.95 cents worth of value when you redeem them towards American Airlines flights.

This means that the sign up bonus for the card is valued at $2,065. Besides this, it also gives you worthwhile perks such as free checked bags, preferred boarding, companion certificates, and in flight discounts. This comes with a card with a comparatively low yearly fee that the company waives during the first year. There is also no foreign currency transaction fee for overseas purchases.

Best Sign-Up Bonus Credit Cards

The United Explorer Business Card offers the best sign up bonuses. After you spend $5,000 over your initial three months, you get 50,000 miles. You also have the chance to earn another 50,000 miles after spending a total of $25,000 over the first six months. This means you can see rewards of from $785 to $1,570 with United Mileage Plus. Besides this, the card is replete with chances for obtaining bonus rewards and useful travel perks.

Best Secured Business Credit Card

Wells Fargo Business Secured Credit Cards will require that you make a cash deposit against the business credit limit which ranges from $500 to $25,000. The card also provides several good rewards programs from which you can select. One of them is their 1.5 percent cash back program on all purchases, hard to beat anywhere[49].

Best Credit Building Cards for Retirement

Retirement means a brand new lifestyle. If your new direction includes daily eating out, travelling, doing home improvements, or taking it easy, there are a variety of best credit cards for your newfound lifestyle. We look at these top credit cards for retirees next.

Best Travel Card

For many retirees, the extra time means more travel. The Capital One Venture Rewards Credit Card delivers big in this regard. You earn double miles on all purchases. The generous sign up bonus included 50,000 miles after spending $3,000 for purchases in your first three months. This equates to $500 worth of travel.

Capital One waives the first year's fee, after which it amounts to $95 annually. These travel rewards are both easy to use and simple to earn. The card gives you the choice of applying your earning to your credit card balance or transferring over miles to one of their numerous travel partners. With no foreign currency transaction fees, it is hard to go wrong with this credit card.

Best Cards for Bulk and Prescription Savings

Prescription drugs consume a lot of retiree resources. The Costco Anywhere Visa Card from Citi helps to lower these burdens with the membership fee of only $60 for Costco covering the credit card fee as well. You receive huge savings on most everything that you purchase at Costco. Their prescription drug prices are among the lowest you will find anywhere, plus you get two percent cash back on all pharmacy spending at Costco.

Best Card for Financing a Large Purchase

When it is time to buy a larger purchase, the best in class card (according to Nerd Wallet) is the U.S. Bank Visa Platinum Card. It gives you fully 18 months of zero percent APR on balance transfers and new purchases, amounting to a free loan for a year and a half on larger purchases. This can cover anything from higher interest rate balance transfers to celebratory trips. With a yearly fee of zero, you can hardly beat this card. It comes with a bonus $600 insurance coverage for your cell phone, allowing two claims totalling $1,200 per year.

Best Card for Everyday Spending

Everyday spending is a great way to earn huge rewards back. As the best in class in this category, American Express wins with its Blue Cash Preferred Card. The annual fee of $95 is offset by the generous welcome offer. Spend $1,000 on purchases over your first three months with the card and you receive a hefty $250 statement credit. You also get a zero percent balance transfer and new purchases offer for a full 12 months. This is a great way to earn rewards for daily needs like gas, groceries, and travel.

Best Card for Dining and Driving

In the category of dining and driving for retirees, Chase wins with its AARP Credit Card. It boasts no annual fee and a generous rewards program of three percent cash back on all restaurants and gas station purchases (one percent on all other categories). Their sign up bonus means that once you spend $500 on any purchases over your first three months with the card, you will get $100 in bonus cash back.

The card pairs well with an AARP membership, though it is not required. The unlimited rewards can be direct deposited to your savings or checking account or applied as a statement credit, whichever you prefer[50].

Environmentally-Friendly Credit Cards

The movement to make your daily spending habits more green is increasingly gaining popularity and traction. Now there are credit cards that are considered to be environmentally friendly. Several banks and well known credit issuers provide these socially conscious accounts. They will donate a certain percentage of your total spending towards environmental causes. We look at four of these credit cards here.

Amazon Watch Visa Platinum

Beneficial State Bank is the issuer of the Amazon Watch Visa Platinum card. A pre-set percentage of all of your purchases will be given to Amazon Watch, the environmental social justice and conservation group. Besides this, they offer a reward program with one for one reward points for each dollar you spend. There is no cap on points earned. You can apply these points for merchandise or towards travel. With no annual fee, this is an environmentally friendly card that is big on brand name recognition.

Credo Mobile

Comenity Bank offers the green Credo Mobile credit card. Each purchase you make allows them to donate 10 cents to revolving batch of not for profit companies working towards environmental sustainability. They will also plant 25 trees in your name if you spend at least $500 over your first 60 days with the account. You also get three rewards points for all grocery store purchases and charitable donations, with one point for all category purchases. You can apply the points towards travel, merchandise, or your statement balance.

Bank of America Defenders of Wildlife Cash Visa

Bank of America brings you this green card that helps endangered and threatened wildlife. For each dollar that you charge, they will donate five cents to green charities. The rewards program gives you a full three percent cash back at gas stations and two percent at grocery stores on your first $1,500 in the combined categories spending, with one percent base on all other charges. If you spend $500 or more in the first three months of the account they will give you another $100 in cash back. As with each of these green credit cards we are considering here, there is no annual fee.

Green America Visa Platinum

Beneficial State Bank/TCM Bank brings you the Green America Platinum Visa card. They donate a percentage for all of your purchases to Green America the environmental group. You also earn one for one reward points for dollars spent with no cap on maximum points earned. You can use these points for merchandise or travel. There is no annual fee with this environmentally responsible credit card.

How to Improve Your Credit

Introduction

Building your credit and credit score up takes some time. Yet the quicker you seriously turn your attention towards the factors that are harming your credit score, the more rapidly your credit scores will rise and improve.

There are a number of practical steps that you can take to get these moving in the right direction. It starts with gaining a history of paying your bills in a timely fashion and paying down your debt. In this chapter we look at practical, actionable steps that you can take to boost your credit.

Make A Commitment to the 90 Day Credit Challenge

I challenge you to commit to a 90 day credit challenge. You should set yourself a 90 day goal to see at least a 100 point improvement in your credit score. You can do this most easily in two ways.

First, pay down any credit card revolving balances that are in excess of 30 percent of your total available credit line. This will significantly improve your score in the second most important   category of credit utilization (which counts for 30 percent of the total score).

Second, make sure you pay all of your monthly balances on time for those three months. This will improve your payment history points, the most important category in credit scoring models (counting for 35 percent of your total). By taking proactive action in both ways, you can see a 100 point improvement or better in your score within three months.

Negative Information Eventually Ages Off Your Report

For your credit report to improve substantially, it will help when the negative or derogatory items drop off. This includes items ranging from too many hard inquiries on your credit report to late payments, charge offs, collections, and bankruptcies. These different detracting features take different amounts of time to disappear from your credit report.

Hard inquiries are the easiest to lose. They only need two years to disappear. Late payments, charge offs, and collections require seven years to drop. They will cause less negative impact as they age. Bankruptcies take from seven to 10 years to disappear. They also impact you less as they age.

You should not let negative items on your credit report keep you from working on improving it, as they will all disappear eventually, and will impact you less each year as they age.

Quick and Easy Approaches That Work Fast

How to Instantly Gain 20 to 30 Points to Your Score

There are two things that you can do to easily and relatively quickly improve your credit score. By making all of your bill payments on time, the credit bureaus will be alerted that you are timely with your monthly payments. This most important category contributes 35 percent of your entire credit score. It needs only a few months for your accounts to all show as timely paid.

Another way to quickly gain 20 to 30 points is to pay your credit card bills down to less than 30 percent of your available credit. By reducing your credit utilization on all accounts to under this figure, you will immediately gain from 20 to 30 points to your score (or more). If you are able to pay the balances down to 10 percent or less, then you will gain still more points almost immediately.

The fastest way to gain major points to your credit score is to reduce those high balances on all cards so that credit utilization is low.

Handling a Dispute On Your Credit Report

You need to regularly check all three of your major credit bureau reports from Equifax, Experian, and TransUnion. It is quite possible that incorrect information on one or more of your reports could be harming your total credit score. Disputing inaccurate or incomplete items with them is easy.

You simply log on to their "file a dispute" pages on their websites at:

TransUnion:
https://www.transunion.com/credit-disputes/dispute-your-credit

Equifax:
https://www.equifax.com/personal/credit-report-services/credit-dispute/

Experian:
https://www.experian.com/disputes/main.html

Here you will be able to open a dispute by providing them with all of the pertinent information on your claim. Be advised that the credit bureaus require up to 30 days to process, research, and correct false information from when you file your dispute. Removing mistakes from your credit report can add significant points back to your score, particularly if the mistakes involve inaccurate late payments or other derogatory information.

Asking for A Lower Interest Rate

If you are carrying monthly balances on your credit cards, you will be able to pay them down faster if you are able to secure a lower interest rate. You can sometimes get these by calling the credit card issuers directly. Tell them you are preparing to pay down your balance, and you would like to ask for a lower interest rate to help you with the process.

They may be more likely to approve your request if you are willing to make a significant token payment while you are on the phone with them.

The Most Effective Solutions Work Better Over Time

There is no way around the fact that credit building solutions which are most effective take time to have an impact. For example, if you start paying your accounts on time today, you will still be feeling the negative effects of late payments from your past for up to seven years.

You can instantly bring your credit utilization down to under 30 percent or even 10 percent, but you can not immediately remove the numbers of hard inquiries from your credit reports. It also takes time to improve your credit mix (10 percent of your score) with varying types of credit like loans and store charge cards, as well as for your credit to age (for 15 percent of your score).

Patience and determination are your best allies in effectively improving your credit scores when they need some work.

Making Use of The Fair Debt Collection Practices Act

The government passed a law that protects you from debt collectors and their predatory practices. This Fair Debt Collection Practices act gives you many rights with the collections of debt. They are not allowed to contact you late at night, harass you with language, or pursue you for a debt that is not yours.

This starts with you being able to limit how and when the debt collectors can contact you. They may not call at either an inconvenient place or time nor tell any third party about your debt. This means that they may not call you at work if you tell them not to, call you before 8 am or after 9 pm, and must not discuss your debt with ay third parties (family, friends, or employers).

If you have an attorney, they must deal with them rather than you. Also, you have the right to tell them to stop contacting you entirely. You must do this in writing for it to be enforced, according to the Fair Debt Collection Practices Act. Fortunately, the Financial Protection Bureau maintains sample letters that you can use to set up your request.

According to the Fair Debt Collection Practices Act, these collectors may not use any deceptive, false, or misleading information in order to collect a debt. If they are behaving too aggressively or abusively, this could be a warning that the debt collector is a scammer.

Determining this can save you the costly errors of paying for a debt that is not yours.

Remember that debt collectors are required by law to answer questions honestly, yet they can choose not to answer them as well. This means that they are not allowed to misrepresent the dollar amount of the debt in question, if it has exceeded the statute of limitations, or their legal avenues if you do not repay the debt.

They also may not threaten to take any of your property or actually take it unless it is allowed by a specific law. Collectors may not collect more than owed on a given debt (which can include fees and interest)[51].

How to Use the Fair Credit Billing Act to Your Advantage

The Fair Credit Billing Act gives you the ability to dispute any charges a credit card issuer claims that you made. The particulars are that you have 60 days from first receiving the bill in order to dispute the relevant charge with the credit card issuer.

Charges have to be in excess of $50 to be eligible.

The date or amount could be wrong, you might not have authorized them, or they could have calculation errors. It may be that you did not receive the service or good promised, which is also grounds for a dispute.

In order to use the act to your advantage, you must do an in writing complaint and mail it to the creditor. If you need a sample letter, go to the Federal Trade Commission's site and use theirs. Your creditor will then have up to 30 days to acknowledge their receipt of this complaint. They are given two full billing cycles to finish their investigation. In this time, the creditor can not charge interest on the charged amount, attempt to collect it, or report you as late to the bureaus.

Such rights only apply to the disputed amount though.

Should the credit's research determine that the dispute charge was not valid, they have to correct the mistake and refund all interest or fees correlated with it. If they determine there was no error, they must explain all findings and provide documentation establishing it. You then have 10 more days to challenge the results of their investigation.

If your card has been stolen or lost, you area allowed to make your disputes over the phone or their website instead of in writing. Your liabilities are always limited to $50 in such a case, though most creditors will pay this too[52].

Understand The Truth in Lending Act

The government passed the Truth in Lending Act back in 1968. It was intended to make sure that you the consumer are fairly treated by lending businesses. You must be correctly informed on the real cost of the credit. The TILA makes lenders reveal all credit terms in a manner that is easy to understand so that you can knowingly comparison shop interest rate terms and conditions.

This act requires that they furnish you with Truth in Lending disclosure statements. These must include your loan's amount, its annual percentage rate, payment schedule, repayment time for the life of the loan, and finance charges (to include late charges, application fees, and prepayment penalties).

These rules only apply to closed end credit accounts, like car loans or mortgages, or open ended accounts such as credit cards.

The act does not restrict the amount of interest a bank charges or if they must approve a given loan. Instead, it makes them reveal in easy to understand terms all costs and fees that come with the loan. This act is also called Regulation Z for short[53].

Issuing a Consumer Statement

In case you have derogatory information contained on your credit report, you possess the rights from the Fair Credit Reporting Act to get a consumer statement attached to your own credit report. The idea behind the statement is to permit you to explain why you got behind on your bills or would not pay a certain bill that you owed. Your reasons could range from a creditor not having kept their arrangement as agreed to having unexpectedly lost your job.

The purpose to such a statement on your credit report is for damage control. It is possible that potential lenders might read the statement and then opt to approve you for credit even with a poor credit rating. After the statement has been attached to your credit report, the bureaus are made to furnish your consumer statement to any individual or organization that requests futures copies of your credit reports[54].

Applications for New Credit and Refinancing Your Loans

When you are applying for new credit, be careful not to make too many requests in a given six month time frame. There is a 10 percent component to your credit score that tracks how many hard inquiries you have received in the last two years.

Too many of these requests will cost you real points from your credit score. This is a penalty amount that you do not have to suffer which you can easily control.

Also be careful how many times you refinance your loans. Besides creating numerous hard hits on your credit report, it gives the idea to creditors that you do not keep your long term contractual arrangements. Each time you refinance, it could increase the amount that you owe, worsening your credit utilization and debt to income ratios, which can cost you significantly on your credit score.

New loans will also reduce your 15 percent category of the score for age of credit, as these loans will water down your average account age when you open them at the same time as you pay off the older account and lose its age contribution.

Using Section 609 to Your Advantage

The Section 609 is a part of the Fair Credit Reporting Act that deals with your rights to obtain copies of your personal credit reports and related information. This section is often confused with section 611, which governs the rights to dispute a charge or debt that you owe.

Section 609 only deals with your rights to get this information that the credit bureaus have on file, not to change it.

The FCRA includes a great deal of information that gives you the ability to dispute information contained in your credit reports in this section 611. If there is information that you feel is unverifiable or incorrect, you can dispute this information.

Because the creditor or lender is required to verify this information, it gives you the opportunity to have a debt or charge removed entirely from your credit report if they can not verify and produce the original documents (such as signed copies of credit applications or cashed checks). In case they would not be able to verify the debt amount without such original documents, they would have to take them off of your credit file[55].

How to Repair Your Credit If Your Identity Has Been Stolen

The most important thing with repairing your credit report after your identity has been stolen is to move fast and with patience. The quicker you are able to find and dispute fraud, the easier it will be to have them removed.

The first thing that you should do is call the credit bureaus and request an immediate freeze on your credit. This will prevent any fraudsters from opening additional accounts.

You should make an unabridged list of all fraudulent accounts. After you have this, go through the steps to dispute each account error on all three of your reports. These mistakes have to be separately reported one by one up to the point that they are all fixed. Trying to report multiple fraudulent errors at one time could cause them to miss some of your disputes. You ought to also write letters of dispute for every fraudulent entry and mail them in. Describe the fraud that has occurred in your letters.

It is imperative that you send the letters using certified mail too. This gives you tracking numbers on when everything is received. Be sure to keep a log of all of your phone calls along with records of electronic and written correspondence. Notes about content and dates of conversations are important to have.

Finally, you should also contact the financial institutions involved directly so that they are aware that there is fraud on your accounts. Do this in writing to fill them in, as you did with the credit reporting bureaus. Send along copies of the police reports and any other documentation that you have as well.

Be aware that this takes time to work through these fraudulent mistakes on your credit reports. It will require persistence and patience to get all of these accounts that are fraudulent removed from your credit report. The more of them that there are the longer it will take[56].

How to Avoid Credit Collection Scams

Many lenders and creditors rely on third party companies in the debt collection business to go after delinquent accounts. Credit card companies use debt collectors like these to pursue charged off accounts all the time. Many debt collectors who call on the phone are legitimate, but there are also scammers posing as collectors who will try to trick you out of money on debt that either does not exist or that has been cancelled or paid off. There are several things to watch for in avoiding such creditor collection scams.

Beware especially any so-called debt collector who asks that you pay them with either a wire transfer or some other method that is non-traceable.

Any legitimate debt collector is sure to accept a range of commonly accepted payments like credit cards, debit cards, or checks. Many nowadays even have online portals on which you can make a payment directly from their website.

Any party asking you to pay by a non-traceable method is highly suspect. These payments that can not be traced are difficult to recover, even with the help of the appropriate authorities.

Another thing to be careful of is when you do not recognize either the account or the creditor involved. In cases where you are positive that you never possessed an account with a company, the chances are high that it is actually a scam.

You should not ever pay off a collection that you do not recognize. Federal rights allow you to demand proof of a debt before you send a debt collector any payment.

The collection company must furnish you with not only proof of the past due debt, but also authorization that they are the ones to collect it. This can be important as many scammers today have gained information about old accounts which consumers actually had and are utilizing such data to trick them out of money.

A faster way to check on a charged off debt is to pull your credit report. Unless the debt account is more than seven years old (at which point it will drop off) it will be there[57].

How to Handle Late Payments

You should avoid late payments on your credit report as much as possible.

Even a single late payment of over 90 days notated can cause your credit score to drop from 90 to 110 points.

There are some things that you can do to address these and clean up your credit report. You should start with asking for a Goodwill Adjustment from your creditor. If you have been timely in your past payment history, the creditor is more likely to accept this request, especially if you have been a customer for some time. In your request, you are asking the creditor to take off the late payment listing in a gesture of customer goodwill as you have generally been a standout customer.

Making such an appeal involves writing the credit card issuer (or other lender) a letter to explain what happened. Perhaps you suffered from an unexpected emergency or situation that caused you to be late. Maybe you want to improve your credit score as much as possible so that you can qualify for a car loan or mortgage.

Provide the details of your personal story so that the agent reading the letter understands your personal situation. A lot of consumers have enjoyed success using this process as so many creditors are not willing to risk you closing the account over one late payment reporting.

There are other cases where the creditor may consent to delete the late payment report if you will sign up to do automatic bill payment. You both win in such a scenario. Your account becomes updated to current and you enjoy the convenience of not needing to remember to pay your bill. This will save you being late in the future. Meanwhile, the creditor is assured of getting payments on time every month.

This method is more successful if you have been late from time to time in the past but are not much delinquent with your account. By proving that you have been capable of making your payments more or less on time, you will enjoy better success with this negotiating tactic. Again, this strategy works best for customers who have been with the creditor longer term.

In the event that you can not get them to remove the late payment willingly or through your own efforts, there are a number of well regarded credit repair companies who will be happy to help you (for a price). We will discuss this option in one of the next chapters.

These companies are staffed by highly experienced and knowledgeable pros that can help you with this and other derogatory listings found on your personal credit report[58].

How to Handle Medical Collections

Medical collections are a pressing issue for many consumers today thanks to inadequacies in the health care system in America. Medical collections are those that specifically pertain to an unpaid medical bill. Such an account sent to collections will probably cause a negative effect on your credit scores. There are a few ways of addressing these accounts in regards to your credit reports. This may involve working with the three major credit reporting bureaus Experian, TransUnion, and Equifax to update any information that is old or inaccurate.

If the account in question is accurate, you should be aware that it may stay on your credit reports for seven and a half years from the point it first went delinquent.

This negative effect will decrease with the age of the collection account. Newer credit scoring models like FICO Score 9 and Vantage Scoring 4.0 place less emphasis on unpaid medical collection accounts than they do on other ones when generating your credit scores.

The federal law NACP makes it illegal for any medical debt to be included on your report until at least 180 days after it was first reported as delinquent to them. The law also stipulates that any bills later paid by insurance must be taken off.

If these scenarios do not pertain to you, you should start by writing the debt collector directly. Insist on your rights to have the debt validated. According to the FDCPA, they must furnish you with proof of your medical collection account debt in order to proceed with their efforts. You must request this in writing within five days of their first effort to contact you about it.

If you do not think you owe this money, it is sensible to demand proof of the debt before you take any other steps. The collector may not be able to verify your debt, in particular if you have already paid the debt or if it mistakenly belongs to someone else. It would make things far simpler to have the collection account taken off of your credit reports if this is the case.

After you have your proof of debt, you can still file a dispute with the individual credit reporting bureaus if you feel there is an error. Any official disputes that you file you must do one by one with every credit bureau, generally through their website is much faster in resolution.

If you have already paid off this debt but it is still illegally contained on your personal credit reports, you should send in documentation showing the payment in full. You could have payment records from the doctor or hospital to include, or a credit card statement or bank statement for proof of form of payment.

The credit bureaus have a month to resolve your issue and respond.

Finally, you should be intimately acquainted with the statute of limitations regarding your medical debts in question. It may be that they will fall off of your credit reports soon enough that you do not need to worry about them. Your legal liability is also limited by the statutes of limitations. Collectors may still trouble you, but they will no longer have the ability to sue you or file judgments past that point.

Be careful about making even small payments on a time limited debt. This can cause it to be revived in some states, which resets the appropriate statute of limitations.

It may be that you actually do not have the money to pay the medical bills. In this case, it is always possible to arrange for a settlement with the debt collector. You would consent to paying a more reasonable amount that you can afford in exchange for them marking the account as settled and ceasing future collection efforts to recover the debt[59].

When Should You Sell Items To Improve Your Credit?

Selling personal items to improve your credit will only help if this gives you more ability to pay down debt under the key 30 percent credit utilization immediately or to make your current and future payments on time. You are losing significant points from your credit score for every credit card on which you maintain a balance over 30 percent, even if you pay this down every month.

This would be a good point to sell some things to pay down debt, as this category of credit utilization counts for 30 percent of your entire score. Getting your credit utilization to less than 10 percent will help improve your score even further.

Remember that the credit scoring models consider not just your average credit utilization score, but also on each individual revolving credit card account as well.

If you are having trouble making all of your credit card payments on time each month, this is costing you dearly in the 35 percent category of timely payment history. You could either pay off several of your balances with money from items sold or at least have money in the bank that you use only for paying your credit card bills.

Late payments reported on your credit report can damage your credit score by as much as from 90 to 110 points, so make it a point to always be on time (or at least not 30 days late, which is the point when most creditors start reporting late payments to the big thee bureaus).

How to Best Handle Debts and Loans

The best way to handle debt and loans is to always pay them on time and not let them grow to more than 30 percent of your available total credit. Not only does this help you with keeping the minimum payments manageable, but it also gives you the crucial points in the credit utilization category.

Your debt to income ratio also should be at 30 percent or less so that it does not become hard to service your debts and loans.

Obviously if you can afford it, the best thing that you can do for your credit score and financial health is to pay off your debt (and loans) in full every month. At the least you can attempt to make larger than minimum monthly payments every month.

Try making a double minimum payment every month to reduce your debt and loans significantly faster.

Remember to apply larger payments to debt with higher interest rates first, as this will reduce the total amount of interest that is assessed and applied to your accounts in the future substantially.

In the next chapter, we will look in more depth at how you can repair your credit on your own, without having to involve the costs of credit repair companies. There are many steps that you can take on your own that will make a significant difference.

Key Takeaways from this Chapter

Set yourself a 90 day goal to see at least a 100 point improvement in your credit score.

* * *

Negative information eventually ages off your report.

* * *

You should not let negative items on your credit report keep you from working on improving it, as they will all disappear eventually, and will impact you less each year as they age.

* * *

The fastest way to gain major points to your credit score is to reduce those high balances on all cards so that credit utilization is low.

* * *

Ask for a lower interest rate. They may be more likely to approve your request if you are willing to make a significant token payment while you are on the phone with them.

* * *

Patience and determination are your best allies in effectively improving your credit scores when they need some work.

* * *

Use the Fair Credit Billing Act. It gives you the ability to dispute any charges a credit card issuer claims that you made.

When you are applying for new credit, be careful not to make too many requests in a given six month time frame.

* * *

Beware especially any so-called debt collector who asks that you pay them with either a wire transfer or some other method that is non-traceable.

* * *

You should not ever pay off a collection that you do not recognize. Federal rights allow you to demand proof of a debt before you send a debt collector any payment.

* * *

Even a single late payment of over 90 days notated can cause your credit score to drop from 90 to 110 points.

* * *

Remember that the credit scoring models consider not just your average credit utilization score, but also on each individual revolving credit card account as well.

* * *

Try making a double minimum payment every month to reduce your debt and loans significantly faster.

How to Repair Your Credit Yourself

Introduction

You have seen ads on television for credit repair or heard them over the radio. The good news is that you do not have to engage a credit repair professional in order to repair your credit. In fact, credit repair companies can not do anything for you to improve your credit that you can not actually do for yourself.

You can save a substantial amount of money (hundreds of dollars) and the time to find the right repair company by doing these activities yourself[60]. In this chapter, we look specifically at the many actions that you can undertake to improve your credit on your own.

The Advantage of Self Repair

There are two main advantages to doing your own credit repair personally without getting a credit repair company involved. The main benefit is all of the costs that you will save. Credit repair companies can not guarantee anything except that you will pay for their services, regardless of how successful they prove to be.

The costs for having them write letters and make calls on your behalf runs well into the hundreds of dollars. They will consistently bill you by the month after they furnish these services.

There is also the possibility that you will hire a company that is a scam. There are many illegitimate operations out there claiming to do credit repair. Watch out for these scamming operations. In the end, they can get you into legal trouble and will only take your money in a best case scenario.

Avoid the time that you need to invest to find a legitimate credit repair company by simply taking these steps to repair your credit on your own.

What to Watch Out For

The Federal Trade Commission warns you that the credit repair industry is littered with scams. This is why you have to be careful in reviewing any potential credit repair company before you engage their services. You should start out by reading Better Business Bureau reviews for the company in question. You can also search through the complaint database of the Consumer Financial Protection Bureau.

The main thing that you need to be watching out for is companies making claims that appear to be too good to be possible. The following claims are all likely proof of a company running a scam:

- They offer to make a new credit profile for you
- Promise to take off negative information that is accurate from your personal credit reports
- Guarantee that they will better your credit
- Ask you to pay before they provide their services

Instead, look for companies that are completely legitimate. Several of these are Sky Blue and Lexington Law[61]. But remember that there are risks if use credit repair companies, which we look at next.

What Is the Risk of Using Credit Repair Companies?

Aside from the real possibility of engaging a credit repair scamming operation, the main risk in hiring a credit repair company is that you will pay hundreds of dollars in fees and not see the results that you hoped for.

Since you can do all of these activities on your own at no cost, there is no reason to pay someone else to do it for you. This is especially the case because there is no guarantee that they will get you the results that you need.

If you must get involved with a credit repair company, try to work with one that offers a 90 day money back guarantee if you are unsatisfied with the results of their efforts.

Step by Step Instructions to Repairing Your Own Credit

There is an easy to follow set of ten steps to follow to repairing your own credit. This is not rocket science, but it does require some patience, persistence, and a little bit of elbow grease. Roll up your sleeves to do the following steps on your own.

1. Obtain the Most Recent Copies of Your Personal Credit Reports

You can not effectively begin to repair your credit until you know what you need to repair in the first place. It is in your credit report where you will find the various mistakes that you have made which have caused you to have bad credit. When you read through it, you should be able to quickly find the derogatory items that are hurting your score. These are listed in their own derogatory items section.

You can easily get your three credit reports for free by going online to the AnnualCreditReport.com website to request your annual free copies. You could order this via the phone or mail if you have plenty of time to wait.

2. Review Your Own Credit Reports for Potential Mistakes

This is actually your best hope to improve your credit right away. You are looking thoroughly for any mistakes that the bureaus might be reporting. For you who own a long credit history, these reports could easily be a few pages in length.

Do not become overwhelmed or discouraged. Take your time to thoroughly go through them and catch any and all mistakes.

Every credit report holds your personal identification information, detailed account history, derogatory information such as collections accounts and past due accounts, public records of bankruptcy, and hard or soft inquiries which others have made on your credit report.

3. Determine What Needs to Be Repaired

There are three kinds of information that may need to be repaired on your credit reports. These start with inaccurate information such as accounts that do not belong to you, falsely reported late payments, and related information. You should carefully read the derogatory remarks section for any late accounts, charge offs, or collection accounts that do not belong there. Also pay close attention for inaccurately listed maxed out accounts which have gone over your credit line.

You can use different color highlighters for the various kinds of information so that you can color code your personal credit repair plan. Each of the different types of information will require different tactics. For example, you would react differently to inaccurate information than to accounts that are past due. This is why using different color highlighters can save you time and help you to quickly find information when you contact (or write letters to) creditors, lenders, or the big three credit bureaus[62].

4. Dispute Your Credit Issues

The next step is to dispute the issues that you have hopefully found needing correction on your three personal credit reports. There is a long running debate on which way you should file these disputes. Online disputes go quicker and are simpler to do, but they do not leave you with a paper trail. You might take dispute screenshots and save these.

If you call the bureaus, you have absolutely no record of your disputes.

As tedious as it may seem, filing disputes via the regular mail comes with a few key advantages. It allows you to include evidence to support your dispute, like cancelled checks that demonstrate making your monthly payments in a timely fashion. It is easy to keep a copy of any dispute letters that you send out this way in a file as well.

A last significant benefit of using traditional mail is that you can send it out through certified mail using return receipt requested. This additional expense will provide you with the hard proof that you need of the day and time that you mailed your dispute.

Credit bureaus are limited to no more than 30 to 45 days to research and rule on your disputes.

It is easy to come up with an effective template for credit report disputes when you will be mailing out multiple disputes. Save this on your computer, and then you can quickly and easily update it for any different consumer credit bureau or individual dispute. Be sure when dispatching your disputes to insert a credit report copy that includes a highlighting of the item being disputed. Also send your documented evidence that proves your case (a copy and not the original).

Be careful not to file more than one or two disputes at a time with the credit bureaus individually, as they may simply decide that you are making frivolous disputes and dismiss them all out of hand.

You should never include more than a single dispute in each letter that you send out to avoid arousing suspicions from the big three credit bureaus.

While you are at it, you might as well send copies of your disputes directly on to the business or bank that originally submitted the information incorrectly to the bureau. Their legal obligations are the same to investigate your filed dispute and update any incomplete, incorrect, or non-verifiable information to your credit report.

5. Follow Up On Your Credit Dispute

Hopefully your dispute will be a success, and you will have the results you desire in an updated and improved credit report. They should also send the alert out to the other big two credit bureaus of the change, but you should follow this up personally. The bureau will dispatch an updated copy of your full credit report to you with the resolution.

If they do not take away the item off of your credit report, they will at the least update it to reveal that you have disputed the negative information. You are then provided the chance and space to include your personal statement on your credit report. While this personal statement will not influence your actual credit score, it does provide more insight into why you disputed the item. Businesses reviewing your credit report manually will see it and consider it.

6. Addressing Past Due Accounts

Past due accounts are devastating on your credit report. They fall into the most crucial category of timely payment history that comprises fully 35 percent of your entire credit score. Because they are so important, it is crucial to avoid multiple past due account listings on your credit reports.

These can cause a negative impact of from 90 to 110 points on your final credit score.

Getting these removed if at all possible is a key task in any process of credit repair. You want to see any and all past due accounts reported to say "paid" if not "current." You can contact the creditors directly about removing past due payment notifications from your credit reports once you have brought them up to date.

As far as any accounts go on which you are behind, you should make them current before they become charged off. Charge offs are among the most serious derogatory account comments. They do not happen until your account is 180 days delinquent. Any of your accounts that are in this delinquency period (but not yet at 180 days late) you can save by paying the full past due amount.

You should know that the more you are behind, the higher your payment to catch up on the account will be. You should call your creditor at once to determine what it will take to bring the account current before they charge it off.

Many creditors will consider removing late penalties when you call them, or at least be willing to spread out the overdue balance over several payments to help you catch up.

Make sure that they understand that you do not want to have the account charged off, but that you require a little help to catch it up. In exchange for catching up on your account, they might consider re-aging your account so that all payments are marked current instead of delinquent. You will have to speak with the creditor in question in order to negotiate such a beneficial outcome.

Accounts that are already charged off you should pay off anyway. The balance is still your responsibility even after the creditor has written them down. Charge offs impact your credit score less as they age, yet having an outstanding balance such as this will make it night on impossible to receive approval on new loans or to obtain new credit. This is why a part of your credit repair task involves paying down charged off accounts.

When you pay this charge off completely down, the creditor will then update your credit report. It will show the account balance as fully paid with a balance of $0.

Unfortunately, the charged off status does not go away until after seven years from the original charge off date.

At least you will have minimized the damage though. You might also settle the charge off amount for less than what you owe. Your creditor will have to agree to work with the proposed settlement and to cancel out the remainder of the original debt.

This settled status will show on your credit report and not drop off for the full seven years. It is possible to negotiate with a creditor to take away the charge off status from your credit report in exchange for paying the full amount.

Be warned that this is not easy to accomplish, but it is worth trying. The most critical step at this stage is to pay down the charge off.

If you are able to get a favorable resolution to the account status, consider this a great and added bonus.

You also need to handle your collection accounts. They would have gone to collections after having been charged off or alternatively after becoming past due a number of months. Accounts that would not typically be shown on your credit report can go to collections too, and at this stage unfortunately they do show up on your credit report. You will be using a nearly identical approach for paying off collections accounts as you did for charged off ones.

Offer to pay in full in exchange for a delete of the negative collection account notation. You might also settle the account for a smaller amount that what you originally owed. Otherwise, the collection notation will remain on your credit report for a full seven years from the date of original delinquency.

7. Reduce Your Credit Card Utilization Ratios and Outstanding Loan Balances

Remember that your credit account utilization is the second largest component of your credit score, worth 30 percent of the whole thing. The larger your balances on each card, the more damage it will do to your credit score. This is an area where you can get almost immediate results with improving your score.

Start with any maxed out and over limit credit card accounts. These cost you important credit score points (on top of the over limit fees you are likely paying as well).

By reducing any over limit or maxed credit cards below their limits, you will be moving that credit utilization ratio down significantly. From this time, make it a point to tackle first one credit card and then another, dropping their balances one by one to less than 30 percent of available credit utilization. Your credit score will be higher when each balance (plus your average balance) is less than the 30 percent ratio.

Under 10 percent is even better and gives you still more score points.

Loan balances are important to consider too. Your credit score algorithm considers your present loan balance versus the original loan amount. The nearer your balances are to the original borrowed amount, the more significantly this impacts your credit score. Credit card balances have the largest effect on your credit scores, so focus all efforts on paying these down to under 30 percent (or even under 10 percent) before you address your loan balances.

8. Prioritize Your Payments Effectively

The truth is that you will only have a limited number of dollars to apply to your credit repair activities every month. This means that you need to prioritize effectively in where you send your payments.

The best strategy is to concentrate on accounts that are nearing past due status. You should make all of these (or as many as possible) current.

Next you will focus on reducing your credit card balances and credit utilization ratios. Your last priority is to make payments on accounts that are already marked as charged off or which have been dispatched to collection agencies. In general, the damage here is already done on these with derogatory remarks likely to remain on your credit report for years (seven), even after you pay them off or settle them.

9. Applying for New Credit

Once you have done everything that you can to address any derogatory items in your credit report, your next step is to focus on having some positive credit information included on your report. Even as late payments do great damage to your score, timely payments on accounts improve it. Once you get a few credit card and loan payments reported as on time, this only helps.

Keep these balances at less than 30 percent and be sure to make all payments on time every month.

You can improve your credit (or rebuild it) through opening up a new credit account. It may be hard to receive approval if you have past delinquencies, so do not make more than one or two applications until you see an improvement in your credit score. This is crucial for keeping the number of hard credit inquiries down.

Every time that you do another application for credit, another hit appears on your credit report under the inquiries final section. Too many of them within a two year period (after which they drop off) will harm your credit score and worsen your chances of becoming approved for new credit.

A good strategy following a rejection from a MasterCard or Visa is to approach a retail store for their store charge card. They are known to approve applicants with either poor or limited credit history. You might also try obtaining a secured credit card with a deposit which you make against the credit limit.

Secured credit cards are extremely useful as you can use them everywhere that MasterCard or Visa is accepted (whereas store cards can only be used at the store or on its website). There are a number of subprime credit cards whose focus is on assisting their customers with rebuilding their credit. Check out their interest rates and fees before you apply, as these will be higher. It is smart to pay down these balances in full every month if they come with high APRs.

10. Salvage As Much As You Can

One thing to keep in mind is that you should not ever sacrifice an account (or several accounts) that are current for accounts that are past due or charged off. The most important thing at this stage is to keep making on time payments for each of your current marked accounts.

You want to hold on to all positive payment history that you can while you are repairing your damaged credit[63].

What is the Credit Repair Organizations Act?

The U.S. Congress passed a law to help protect you the consumer in 1996 called the Credit Repair Organizations Act. It mandates that firms which provide credit repair services must communicate with and advertise honestly with potential customers and clients.

This CROA exists in the context of a bigger set of statutes entitled the Consumer Credit Protection Act. CROA is intended to safeguard consumers from firms that charge fees while falsely promising to have accurate, negative items taken off of their credit reports. It also protects from promises to drastically boost lower credit scores which are predicated upon accurate information.

For example, the CROA outlaws these firms from pledging to provide consumers with a new start including a brand new credit profile. It mandates that the firms must inform consumers that they can repair their own credit without assistance. Thanks to the CROA, these credit repair firms can not assess major fees to clients before they have delivered their credit repair services[64].

Instructions for Filling Out Dispute Letters with the Credit Bureaus

The big three credit bureaus all accept dispute filing online (Experian is only accepting online submissions nowadays). You can get the instructions for filing online disputes by clicking here.

When you write to the credit bureaus and mail them the letter, it is critical that you inform them clearly of information that you believe is incorrect. Send along copies of documents which provide evidence of your claims.

Next, you need to include a copy of your credit report that has any items you are disputing circled. After writing the letter to accompany these enclosures, be sure to send your letter using certified mail with return receipt requested. This will allow you to document correspondence with the credit bureau.

Make sure to keep a copy of your enclosures and dispute letter!

On the next 3 pages are three sample dispute letters that you can use in your communication with the credit bureaus:

First Sample Letter[65]:

Date
Your Name
Your Address
Your City, State, Zip Code

Complaint Department
Name of Credit Bureau
Address
City, State, Zip Code

Dear Sir or Madam:

I am writing to dispute the following information in my file. The items I dispute also are encircled on the attached copy of the report I received.

This item (identify item(s) disputed by name of source, such as creditors or tax court, and identify type of item, such as credit account, judgment, etc.) is (inaccurate or incomplete) because (describe what is inaccurate or incomplete and why). I am requesting that the item be deleted (or request another specific change) to correct the information.

Enclosed are copies of (use this sentence if applicable and describe any enclosed documentation, such as payment records, court documents) supporting my position. Please reinvestigate this (these) matter(s) and (delete or correct) the disputed item(s) as soon as possible.

Sincerely,

Your name

Enclosures: (List what you are enclosing)

Second Sample Letter[66]:

Full Name

Mailing Address:

Date of Birth

{If Sending to Experian: P.O. Box 4500, Allen, TX 75013}

{If Sending to Equifax: P.O. Box 740256, Atlanta, GA 30374-0256}

{If Sending to Transunion: Consumer Disputes, P.O. Box 2000, Chester, PA 19016}

{Date}

RE: Investigation Request to Delete Credit Inquires

To whom it may concern,

In accordance with the Fair Credit Reporting Act Section 611 (15 U.S.C. § 1681I), I am practicing my right to challenge questionable information that I have found on my personal credit report. I do not recognize the information listed below and request that you investigate the source of these accounts and ascertain that the creditor had a permissible purpose, and is able to verify my complete file information including full name, address, date of birth and SSN#.

INCORRECT ACCOUNT INFORMATION

The accounts below are reporting incorrectly please investigate these:

1. {Creditor Name} {ac#}   {Reason for Dispute}
2. {Creditor Name} {ac#}   {Reason for Dispute}
3. {Creditor Name} {ac#}   {Reason for Dispute}

INCORRECT CREDIT INQUIRIES

I am disputing the following inquiries which I did not authorize:

1. {Creditor Name} {inquiry date}
2. {Creditor Name} {inquiry date}

REMOVE INCORRECT PERSONAL INFORMATION
I am disputing the following personal information that is showing for me which is incorrect:

1. Incorrect SSN {xxx-xx-xx xx }
2. Incorrect Address { insert address}
3. Incorrect Name Variations { Insert name}

UPDATE PERSONAL INFORMATION
Also please update the following information which I saw your credit bureau to be missing or incomplete:

1. Personal current address {insert correct address}
2. My proper full { insert your correct full name, if the bureau has listed it incorrectly}
3. My date of birth { insert date of birth, if bureau has it listed incorrectly}
4. My current employment info { insert employer name, address and your position, if the bureau is missing this info}

I am allowing you 30 days to complete this investigation after which I authorize you to mail me my updated credit reports along with the investigation results

Truly,

{Name}

{Signature}

Third Sample Letter[67]: (from the Federal Trade Commission)

Your Name
Your Address
Your City, State, Zip Code

Date

Complaint Department
Company Name
Street Address
City, State, Zip Code

Dear Sir or Madam:

I am writing to dispute the following information in my file. I have cir-cled the items I dispute on the attached copy of the report I received.

This item [identify item(s) disputed by name of source, such as credi-tors or tax court, and identify type of item, such as credit account, judgment, etc.] is [inaccurate or incomplete] because [describe what is inaccurate or incomplete and why]. I am requesting that the item be removed [or request another specific change] to correct the informa-tion.

Enclosed are copies of [use this sentence if applicable and describe any enclosed documentation, such as payment records and court docu-ments] supporting my position. Please reinvestigate this [these] mat-ter[s] and [delete or correct] the disputed item[s] as soon as possible.

Sincerely,
Your name

Enclosures: [List what you are enclosing.]

Remember to only address one issue per letter, as the credit bureaus may throw out your entire investigation as superfluous otherwise.

Make sure to follow up your dispute with the credit bureau if you do not hear from them within the 30 to 45 days in which they are required to research and notify you of their decision!

The Section 609 Credit Repair Secret

As we noted before, there are a pair of sections in the Fair Credit Reporting Act that you can use to your advantage in cleaning up your own credit report. These are the powerful secret sections of 609 and 611. Section 609 gives you the right to know what is contained within your credit report. It is section 611 that provides you with the means of disputing the information found in your reports.

Any information that you believe is either incorrect or unverifiable you may dispute.

The burden of proof then falls on the creditor or lender to substantiate this original debt. If they can not do this, then you will be able to get the charges or debt taken completely off of your credit report. They must send you a copy of the original documents (cashed checks or signed credit applications) in order to substantiate the debt.

If they can not do this, then the debts come off from your credit report entirely[68]. This is powerful and actionable intelligence in your efforts to repair your own credit report.

How to Handle Delete Collections and Charge-Offs

Getting collections and charge offs deleted from your credit report is not an easy task, but it has been done. It does not take a professional to do it either. The method starts with contacting the original creditor in the case of a charge off or the collector if the account has been sent out to third party collections. You then negotiate with them to remove the collection or charge off from your credit report in exchange for paying the full amount while on the call.

If they will not do this, then you can try settling the debt for a smaller amount than what you originally owed. Most collectors will agree to a settlement, and then they will mark your credit report account as "settled and paid." This is a second best alternative to having the derogatory item completely removed, but it does help mitigate the damage to your credit score and will certainly look better to future potential lenders and creditors who will be going through your credit report and taking careful note of such important details.

Knowing Your Credit Utilization Ratio

The single easiest thing for you to control with your credit score is your credit utilization rate. You should always be aware of this figure on all of your accounts as well as on average.

The credit bureaus and scoring algorithms start penalizing you heavily when it exceeds 30 percent even on a single account.

To find your credit utilization ratio, you simple divide your total credit outstanding over your total available credit for each account. For example, if you have $200 charged on a $500 credit card limit, then you are using 40 percent of your credit on that particular account.

An easy and quick way to pick up points in your score is to pay this ratio down below 30 percent on each account. It will take only a month or at most two for this information of a lower ratio to be updated on your credit report. No other actions you can take will have such a rapid and dramatic improving effect on your credit score, since this credit utilization makes up fully 30 percent of your total possible score.

Improve Your Payment History

Another critical task you need to do in fixing your credit reports is to get your payment history showing timely on as many accounts as possible (and ideally on all of them). If you are only showing a single late payment or two, you may be able to negotiate with your creditors in a Goodwill Letter for them to remove these late payment remarks in exchange for signing up for automatic bill payment with your checking account.

Be sure to keep all accounts current going forward, as this amounts to the largest single component of your credit score for 35 percent. Building up a timely payment history requires a good six months, so this is something that you want to start on right away, in particular if the creditors opt not to remove any damaging late payment remarks (that take seven years to fall off of your credit report otherwise).

The Best Way to Deal With Bankruptcies

There are two key ways that you need to handle bankruptcies on your credit report. Both of these involve tackling the bankruptcy head on instead of attempting to hide from it. One silver lining in a bankruptcy is that it erases your delinquent and outstanding account balances. Your credit report will display $0 balances on any accounts that were successfully discharged via the bankruptcy.

The first action is to ensure that your credit report correctly reflects these effects of your bankruptcy. Sometimes creditors will stubbornly keep reporting the negative account information even after your bankruptcy discharge. This is why you need to routinely check out your credit report.

You can use a free third party credit report/score service like Credit Karma or Discover It to do this as often as you like. Checking it at least once a month in this situation is a good idea.

It will not cause you any hard credit inquiries.

Should you find out that one or more of your creditors are showing discharged debts as active (with balances outstanding), then you need to talk with the appropriate credit reporting bureau right away. A more proactive approach is to send every agency copies of your discharge as soon as you receive it. This will alert them to the fact that they are not to report additional information on all included accounts.

When you do come across reporting errors, you are within your rights to send out disputes to the three credit bureaus. They must address them within 30 to 45 days.

The second action to take is to continue paying all of your non-discharged accounts on time. Not every one of your accounts will fall under the discharge order. Student loans are one prime example that can not be discharged. These active accounts will keep affecting your credit score, so be sure to pay all existing accounts and loans in a timely fashion.

Just because an account does not yet show on your credit report is not a good reason to ignore it. Should you fall behind on payments, the accounts will be reported to the bureaus and appear tragically as if by magic. Your overarching goal is to let creditors see that your financial problems are in the past[69].

The Best Way to Deal With Foreclosures

Foreclosures have a devastating impact on your credit report. The good news is that these are easier to get removed than other derogatory items. Lenders have made countless mistakes with foreclosures in the past, forcing some financial institutions to have to offer restitution to consumers when they mismanaged their foreclosures.

Among these errors were rubber stamping documents and not pursuing the proper procedure required by foreclosure law. This is why it is easier to get such records completely removed from your credit report today.

For one thing, the lender may not even possess the necessary records. Many original lenders went bankrupt during the Global Financial Crisis and Great Recession of 2007 to 2009. Countless original documents necessary to verify the mortgage disappeared in the chaos. Many such mortgages and foreclosure rights have been sold on to new banks, creating a paperwork nightmare for the banks.

Such sales had the unintended side effect of causing banks to fail in their task of accurate record keeping. If the bank that was listed on your credit report has gone out of business, the new bank will likely not be able to verify the foreclosure.

All information like this in your credit file that they can not verify with the necessary documentation has to be removed by law.

Armed with this background knowledge, you should write to your foreclosing lender directly. If the credit bureaus will not remove the foreclosure, go straight to the source of the derogatory information.

Request that they take off the entry because of mistakes. Allow them a 30 day deadline to do so before you take further action.

In many cases, the foreclosing bank will not be able to produce the original documentation and records to verify your foreclosure. They might also decide it is not worth the time and effort to track them down. In either scenario, they will likely simply choose to remove your foreclosure remark from your credit report[70].

This is worth the considerable time that it may take on your part to make the phone calls, write the letters, and follow up on, since it requires seven years for a foreclosure to drop off of your credit report otherwise.

The Best Way to Deal With IRS Tax Liens

Thanks to the credit bureau reforms of 2017 and 2018, tax liens no longer appear in your credit report under the public records section. This does not magically make them go away in reality though.

They do not impact your credit score any longer, but they will affect other areas of your financial life.

The easiest way to be rid of a tax lien on a home or property is to pay the bill in full. If you can not do this, then contact the IRS directly about settling it for an amount that you can pay. In many cases, they will prefer to receive a part of the tax debt rather than nothing.

You may also apply for a lien withdrawal. Such an action would remove the public Notice of Federal Tax Lien. The end result is to show that the IRS is no longer vying with your other creditors to take possession of your house. Ultimately, if you are able to sell your house then the lien will simply disappear on its own. In any case, it is no longer impacting your credit history or score.

How do I Consolidate My Loans?

We have talked in detail about consolidating credit card bills so far but not yet really looked at consolidating loans. The idea behind consolidating your loans is to gather multiple loans in order to combine them into one larger loan. This provides a primary benefit of reducing the hassles of doing several payments every month. It diminishes your chances of accidentally missing or being late for a loan payment. If you are writing four to five different checks a month, this is entirely possible. A single payment each month is easier to remember to mail.

Only consolidating loans however will not reduce your interest costs or payment schedule.

This is because a typical consolidation involves a new interest rate that is the weighted average of your combined prior loan interest rates. It could even lengthen the life time of your loan to consolidate depending on fees and new payment amount. Refinancing on the other hand would allow you to take the existing loans to reduce the old interest rates for a lower new one.

The lower this rate proves to be, the less you will pay in interest for the loan overall[71]. You can get a refinancing or consolidation loan from most banks and financial institutions. They do require average to good credit to be approved.

Accessing Information from Specialized Bureaus

Besides the big three credit reporting bureaus of Experian, Equifax, and TransUnion, there are also some specialized consumer bureaus that contain important information which can definitely affect your finances. You can gain access to these if you need to. The most important of these for most consumers is the ChexSystems. We look at these in the last section of this chapter.

ChexSystems

When you go into a bank to apply for a new bank account, over 80 percent of banks will pull your report from ChexSystems to learn if you have any prior history of misusing bank accounts. Such information remains in their systems for five years after the fact.

It will influence their approval or rejection decision for your new account.

Chex Systems is actually a national consumer reporting agency that manages information on the use of checking and savings accounts. If you have failed to pay a fee or bounced a check, this information will be contained in your ChexSystems file. The good news is that you can obtain both your report and score from the agency at no cost.

The report is the most useful information to have. It provides you with the back story on the reason a bank might have turned down your new account request. You are able to obtain a free copy of this report each year. You can simply request your report online by filling out this consumer disclosure form. They will send you the report which should arrive in only five business days or faster[72].

CLUE Reports

CLUE is the claims information report database created and maintained by LexisNexis the international giant consumer reporting agency. They hold as much as seven years worth of your personal property and automobile claims history.

This report will have your personal information including all of the following: your name and date of birth, policy number, type and date of loss, claim amount the firm paid out, description of the property that was covered, and your property address. The insurance companies report all claims where they pay out, deny, or establish a file on a claim.

These CLUE reports are important where insurance is concerned. A potential insurer will likely pull your CLUE report if you ask for an insurance quote or make a full application for coverage. They are interested in your history of claims in determining what coverage they will offer you and at what cost. Their research demonstrates a consistent relationship between prior paid claims and future reported claims.

You are able to get your free annual copy of your CLUE report courtesy of the Fair Credit Reporting Act. You can request this from LexisNexis online at: Request your personal report online (www.lexisnexis.com) or by calling their consumer center[73] at 866-312-8076.

Judicial Judgments

It used to be that judicial judgments showed up on your three credit reports. This practice ended in 2017/2018 when the big three bureaus eliminated all judgments from your reports and scoring algorithms. Bankruptcy is the only public record that shows up on your credit reports anymore. In order to find out if there are any other judgments against you nowadays, you would need to order a copy of your public records from the county in which you reside. You can do this in person at the courthouse or by going to their website online.

Utilities History

Your utility payment history will appear on your credit report. If you are behind on payments or have charge offs with any utilities, then it will show up here. This is something that you should keep a lookout for on your credit report. Timely utility payment history will not appear on your report. It is only if you fall meaningfully behind that there will be reports made to the big three consumer credit reporting bureaus[74].

Rental Background Check

Rental background checks are not simple reports compiled by a consumer reporting agency. Instead, they comprise information mostly found on your consumer credit report, such as your personal details and address, credit score, and listings of any collections, inquiries, and bankruptcies.

They also include your employment history, public records, criminal records, and eviction records. Most of this other information the organization which is conducting the rental background check will obtain from your public records or from the application that they make you fill out for them.

If you have been repeatedly delinquent on rent payments or not paid some final rent amount in the past, there is a good chance that it will show up as reported to the credit bureaus under derogatory information. Experian RentBureau is a separately maintained report that Experian keeps on timely and late rent payments.

You can request a fee report from them by contacting them on their website at: http://www.experian.com/rentbureau/renter-credit.html

Medical Insurance History

Your medical and insurance histories may not be given out without your expressed written permission. Because of this, there is no single national medical records database or report containing this information. Instead, individual doctor's offices and hospitals each have some of your medical insurance information.

Thanks to the Data Protection Act of 1998, no doctor will comply with a request from an insurer to reveal your medical records unless you agree in writing. The state health information exchanges are the closest things to a national database or report on your medical insurance history. You can contact the one for your state to see if they have your information available in a report to obtain a copy should you require it.

In the next chapter we will consider and look at how to use a credit repair service in order to effectively fix your credit history and improve your critical personal credit score.

Key Takeaways from this Chapter

Do not become overwhelmed or discouraged reading through your credit report. Take your time to thoroughly go through them and catch any and all mistakes.

* * *

Credit bureaus are limited to no more than 30 to 45 days to research and rule on your disputes.

* * *

You should never include more than a single dispute in each letter that you send out to avoid arousing suspicions from the big three credit bureaus.

* * *

Many creditors will consider removing late penalties when you call them, or at least be willing to spread out the overdue balance over several payments to help you catch up.

* * *

The best strategy is to concentrate on accounts that are nearing past due status. You should make all of these (or as many as possible) current.

* * *

You want to hold on to all positive payment history that you can while you are repairing your damaged credit.

* * *

Make sure to keep a copy of your enclosures and dispute letter!

* * *

Any information that you believe is either incorrect or unverifiable you may dispute.

* * *

The credit bureaus and scoring algorithms start penalizing you heavily when it exceeds 30 percent even on a single account.

* * *

When you do come across reporting errors, you are within your rights to send out disputes to the three credit bureaus. They must address them within 30 to 45 days.

* * *

All information in your credit file that they can not verify with the necessary documentation has to be removed by law.

* * *

Request that they take off the entry because of mistakes. Allow them a 30 day deadline to do so before you take further action.

* * *

Tax liens do not impact your credit score any longer, but they will affect other areas of your financial life.

CHAPTER

13

How To Use A Credit Repair Service

There are four main reasons that you may choose to go down this route. The first is that credit repair companies will proactively take charge of your situation. These are dedicated, trained, and highly experienced professionals who have prior working relationships with both the credit bureaus and creditors and who possess a track record of resolving consumer credit issues.

Secondly, using the credit repair organizations saves you huge amounts of time. The process is typically both tedious and demandingly long. Knowledge of a number of laws and back and forth communications will be required on every single item that you question on your credit report. Some scenarios may even involve you having to challenge original creditor claims, or to deal with collection agencies, the big three credit bureaus, or all of these groups together.

When you pay for this important service, you give authorization for the pros to handle your credit reports, obtain information, write the letters, keep the communication records, and handle all of the considerable follow up work. This frees up considerably your schedule and takes the worry from your mind.

Remember a third reason in that these repair services are expertly versed in and knowledgeable of the relevant credit laws. This helps them to obtain the improvements in credit reports that you are seeking. They know how to work the laws and system for your benefit.

Credit repair services understand how to operate under the FCRA Fair Credit Reporting Act, the FDCPA Fair Debt Collections Practices Act, the FCBA Fair Credit Billing Act, and various other consumer protection laws.

Finally, you will reap longer term gains by paying manageable monthly fees to credit repair companies over several months. If you use a company which provides results in repairing and boosting your credit, this will continue to save you money for the rest of your financial life.

Every time you take out a mortgage or a car loan, your interest rates will be lower, leading to significantly less interest paid out over the life of your loans.

Spending the money today to better your credit score will eventually pay you back handsomely versus those who do not take the time to address inaccurate and unsubstantiated credit report data. It may even lead to better apartment rentals and job offers in the future. You simply can not afford to put off or ignore entirely improving your poor credit.

With 79 percent of all credit reports riddled with mistakes, it is entirely in your rights to have the big three credit bureaus prove the data or remove it entirely.

The Basics of Credit Repair Services

The credit repair process is as much of an art as it is a science, and no two individuals' time requirements will be the same. It will always require at the very least 30 days to do, but can easily take up to six months and even longer. This time frame all depends on the prior condition of your credit profile.

If you only have a couple of inaccurate items that are holding back your score, this can be fixed far quicker than a lengthy history of defaults and delinquencies can. If you are prepared for it to require three months, then you will likely not be too disappointed if it runs another month or two over this.

What will happen if all of the negative items on your credit reports are accurate?

Usually such accurate negative information can not be taken off of a credit report. You could pay off a delinquent or charged off account, and this would result in the account status simply being updated to reveal that it has been paid in full. Unfortunately, accurate derogatory remarks like charge offs and late payments will follow your credit report around for seven years from the first delinquency date. That is of course unless you employ a skilful credit repair company which is practiced in negotiating to have such remarks removed by the original creditors and lenders.

There are extenuating circumstances in which such negative items can be removed. If the creditor made a billing error somewhere, then you can force the creditor to contact the credit reporting bureaus to take the account completely off of your credit report. If you challenge the debt and the creditor can not substantiate it with original documents that prove its validity, they will also be forced to get it removed.

As a general rule, this is far more likely with a home foreclosure than it is with a credit card bill[75].

How Much Do Credit Repair Services Cost?

Each credit repair service will have its own price or tier of pricing to work on your credit reports. In general, they will charge you by the month and only after they have completed the months' work. According to NerdWallet, the average professional credit repair service costs around $100 per month[76].

Other companies may charge a one time, lump sum amount of $300 for six months of credit repair. If you have a lot of items that need to be addressed on your credit profile, you might save money by paying such a lump sum, as more than six months of credit repair services could otherwise cost you in excess of $600 (and this amount of time to fix credit reports is not unheard of).

You could pay as little as $30 per month to one of these companies, but beware that you generally get what you pay for with credit repair (as well as in most areas of life).

How Do Credit Repair Companies Work?

Legitimate credit repair companies do many things on your behalf to improve your credit reports and scores. They will usually begin services by asking for current copies of your credit reports from all of the big three consumer credit reporting bureaus Experian, Equifax, and TransUnion. Once they have obtained these complete reports, they will then go carefully through your reports looking for any derogatory remarks such as delinquent accounts and charge offs, collections accounts, and bankruptcies.

Their next step is to create a specific plan for the best way to dispute any errors and negotiate with your individual creditors with the ultimate goal of getting such items removed. Such a plan of attack could include sending out letters that make requests for debt validation, dispatching dispute letters for inaccurate negative comments, and making contacts (in writing) to collectors ordering them to cease and desist their collections efforts against you.

These companies will also encourage you to get proactive as part of their plan. They will recommend that you apply for one or more new credit accounts in order to have new positive information updates included on your credit reports. Only be sure that you are able to make timely consistent monthly payments on any new accounts added so that you do not make your fragile credit situation any worse. It is not always a sensible approach to seek our more credit that you do not need[77].

Also beware any credit repair service plans that are big on trying to get accurate negative information removed from your reports. Unless they uncover accounts where the creditors will not be able to verify and validate the original debts, they will not be able to get these removed from your reports (absent negotiating to pay them in full).

Is Credit Repair Legal in All 50 States?

Credit repair services are legal in every state of the U.S. Thanks to the Fair Credit Reporting Act, you have the right to make certain that all of the information contained in your personal credit files is completely accurate. This does not mean that every credit repair company under the sun is above board though. In fact the opposite is more likely to be the case.

Thanks to the two primary credit repair federal laws the Fair Credit Reporting Act and the Credit Repair Organizations Act (and other important legal sections 609 and 611), your rights to fix credit mistakes in your reports are guaranteed as a consumer. Each state also maintains its own host of statutes for regulating credit repair services and the industry as a whole[78].

How Can You Verify the Legitimacy of a Credit Repair Company?

The easiest and fastest way to check out a credit repair company's legitimacy and all around reputation is to go to the Better Business Bureau website and enter their name. The BBB maintains ratings and complaints on these companies which can save you the cost and heartache of getting involved with a credit repair scammer.

If you want to spend more time, you can familiarize yourself with the Credit Repair Organizations Act to know what signs to look for in a crooked company which is propagating scams. You should always strenuously avoid those credit repair companies that break the law by asking for payment upfront in advance, who promise to make you a new credit identity, or who guarantee that your credit score will rise as a result of their efforts.

Besides the monthly fee to work on your credit reports and profile, most legitimate companies will also assess a one time customer intake fee to get started. This helps them to cover the costs of obtaining all three of your full credit reports. The customer intake fee could easily run as much as from $100 to $200, depending on the company and its procedures.

The Best Five Credit Repair Companies in 2020

It is always a good idea to go with one of the top credit repair companies to ensure that you get legitimate credit repair services at a fair price. To make finding these easier, we have ranked and considered the top five credit repair companies for 2019 here for you next. All of them are well-respected and – regarded in the industry and by their existing and past customers.

1. Lexington Law

Lexington Law is something like the gold standard of traditional credit repair companies. This stems from its long years of proven and vast customer experience in the field that date back to more than 25 years. This group also gets major points for being a law firm that specializes exclusively in credit repair. They have the largest number of successful results and clients to share, with more than nine million derogatory items taken off from client credit reports in the year 2016 alone.

The company has assisted over half a million clients with credit repair since 2004. We love that Lexington provides three tiers of service, specializing in the Premier Plus program that offers a broad variety of features including providing personal finance tools and tracking your FICO score. You can cancel at any time with Lexington Law.

2. Sky Blue Credit Repair

A close second to Lexington in many rankings of credit repair firms is Sky Blue Credit Repair. They have been helping clients since 1989 and offer a free consultation. Their simplicity is among the most appealing features of this firm. Sky Blue offers their famous flat rate payment plan that sets a fixed price for an individual or a couple.

Credit repair is the only service which they offer, making them extremely laser focused on this work. Sky Blue offers 15 items disputed per month and allows you to easily track your credit repair progress online 24 hours per day, seven days per week. With a full 90 day complete money back guarantee, you really have nothing to lose using Sky Blue (except your negative credit report items). The company boasts fast results for most clients appearing in only 30 days.

You can get started with a very reasonable $79 and may cancel or even pause your membership at any point in the process.

3. The Credit Saint

The Credit Saint is more than just a cool sounding company name. They deliver credit reports from each of the big three consumer reporting bureaus at the conclusion of a billing cycle so that you can literally see the progress of their ongoing credit repair. With three different tiers of service, Credit Saint provides its 90 day, 100 percent money back guarantee for all clients.

Their one time fee is $99 but they offer monthly fees starting at under $80 and no contract to sign.

The firm has been around for 15 years and has demonstrated its penchant for online transparency, an easy to follow credit repair process, and extremely competitive services and prices in this time. Their wealth of information available to all on the company website ensures that you are able to fully investigate all that they offer before committing to become a client. Their website might be the easiest to navigate of all the top five credit repair companies.

With a simple click, prospective customers are able to view the details of all three of the company credit repair plans, including what each provides and what it costs. You can have their help for as little as less than $60 per month, making them among the most affordable of the best-rated credit restoration firms.

4. The Credit Pros

The Credit Pros use an intuitive system of payment that provides their clients with the ability to attack individual derogatory credit items. They also give you the choice to go with a more traditional payment plan per month, which usually amounts to a less expensive option in the long run. In this monthly plan, you get unlimited dispute filing, many different types of letters that they will write for you, and a helpful web portal available to you 24 hours per day, seven days per week to follow your individual progress.

Whatever way you choose to pay, the Credit Pros are the most expensive of the big five credit repair companies. Yet you get what you pay for as always, which includes individual, private consultation, cease and desist letters to collectors, and unlimited disputes. One downside of the company is that their services are not offered in all 50 states as of time of publication.

5. The Credit People

A relative late comer to the big five credit repair firms is The Credit People. Founded only in 2001, they still have two decades of experience in helping you with your bad credit profiles. They have already assisted more than 100,000 individuals in raising their credit scores.

The firm is huge on high quality customer service and this is their focus, in providing past and current clients with unrivalled benefits. Among these advantages are free credit score and credit report summaries, less expensive fees (including an only $19 one time upfront fee), and 24 hour full access to your online account portal. The company is committed to score-driven results, and goes above and beyond the usual means of disputing with the big three credit bureaus to achieve these.

They do not have a contract and offer a flat monthly fee of under $80 per month. Their satisfaction guarantee ensures that you will only pay for results with which you are fully satisfied. This concludes with three credit scores and reports from Experian, Equifax, and TransUnion at no additional charge to you. The company promises to help you get the highest potential credit score that you can achieve personally.

Removal and Deleting of Specific Entries

Getting specific derogatory items removed from your credit report is an essential part of credit repair and improving your personal credit score. There are four different ways to approach this successfully, and any good credit repair company will likely pursue as many of them as necessary (and even concurrently) to get your desired results.

1. Submit a Dispute to the Big Three Credit Bureaus

Your credit repair company will likely start by leveraging the Fair Credit Reporting Act. This Federal law details the kinds of information that the credit bureaus can list on your report and for what amount of time (typically seven years). Because of the stipulation in the FCRA that you possess the rights to a credit report that is accurate, credit repair companies will file disputes on any errors with the appropriate credit bureaus first.

2. Dispute with the Original Creditor who Reported the Remark to the Credit Bureaus

A good credit repair company will likely simultaneously work a second approach to having the items removed from your credit report by going around the credit bureaus to directly address the creditor regarding the error on your report. This could be a debt collector, bank, or credit card issuer who they are contacting.

They will send out a physical letter that forces the creditor or lender to begin an investigation as a credit bureau would. It will require that they verify the debt with original documentation. If they can not substantiate it, then it will have to be removed from your credit report altogether.

3. Dispatch a Pay for Delete Compromise to Your Creditor

The credit repair companies have several other tricks up their sleeves if the derogatory information is both correct and can be verified as a legitimate debt. They know that the credit bureaus will never take off such information even when it is disputed (once their investigation affirms the debt and its accuracy). So they will go to the original creditor and make them a negotiating offer that is hard to refuse.

Pay for delete simply means that the creditor will allow you to pay off your delinquent account in exchange for having all negative remarks regarding the account itself deleted from your credit files. There are creditors who will be only too happy to accept such an offer, which really costs them nothing but a few minutes of their time and gets them paid back in full.

4. Pursue a Goodwill Request for Deletion

If you are not much behind on an account, or if you have already paid off the debt, then you have given up your negotiating power for the credit repair company to offer the Pay for Delete. Instead, they can appeal to the mercy of the creditor in a request for goodwill deletion.

Here is how this works in practice. The credit repair company will write a professional and heartfelt letter to your original creditor explaining the reasons that you were behind on the account and reminding them that you were generally a timely paying customer. They will request as a gesture of goodwill that the creditor adjust the reports on the account to be more favorable.

Creditors are not required to do this, and some will outright refuse. But then again, it costs nothing but some time and letters to make such a request. Another advantage to working with credit repair companies is that they will be able to speak to the right people at the lender who can make such a positive decision on your behalf[79].

Removal of Late Payments, Collections, and Charge Offs

The more serious the derogatory item on your credit report, the harder it will be for your credit repair company to get it completely removed. They will likely find that correctly reported collections and charge offs can only be removed by the use of tactic number three above with a Pay for Delete compromise.

This is the only real leverage that you have with accounts that are so delinquent that they have already been charged off and/or sent out to a third party collections agency. Your credit repair service can offer to make the full original past due payment amount (trying to negotiate away some of the charges and late fees in the process) in exchange for them striking all associated negative account remarks from your credit report.

Again, this will be much easier to negotiate for simple late payments than it will be for charge offs and especially collection accounts (which are doubly reported negatively under both charge offs and as collection accounts).

Removal of Bankruptcies

No matter how good a credit repair company may be, it is not possible for them to get a discharged bankruptcy removed from your credit files. These simply have to fall off after the stipulated from seven to 10 years time frame. They can get inaccurate information concerning the bankruptcy updated and amended however.

You should check over this section of your credit report and consult with your credit repair company to see if any information needs to be corrected here. Bankruptcies on credit reports may seem like they are permanent fixtures, but their impact becomes less damaging with every passing year from the date of discharge.

Removal of Repossessions and Foreclosures

Repossessions pertain to loans on cars, trucks, and boats, while foreclosures relate to houses on whose mortgage you have defaulted. In both cases, the credit repair company knows that your best chances of getting these devastating derogatory remarks removed from your credit report center on challenging the original creditor to verify and validate the debt. Thanks to the Global Financial Crisis of a decade ago, many of the original lenders went bankrupt themselves.

As a result, in the ensuing confusion, many mistakes were made and a huge number of original documents were lost forever. If your lender on your loan or mortgage is long gone, then your credit repair company has a decent chance of successfully challenging the creditor to produce the original debt documents. If they can not show original signed applications or other original proof of the debt, then they will have no choice but to contact the credit bureaus and have these accounts removed from your reports entirely.

Removal of Judgments

Thanks to that rarest of occurrences when the three major credit bureaus agreed on providing relief to consumers (as they did back in 2017-2018), judgments and liens (including tax liens) no longer appear anywhere on your credit reports, nor do they impact your personal credit scores. There is no longer any need to have them removed. Just because they are not listed on your credit profile any longer does not mean that you do not still owe the debt. It also does not stop the creditors from trying to collect one way or another.

Removal of Inquiries

Legitimately listed hard inquiries on your credit reports can not be removed either by you or any credit repair organization. They will drop off naturally after no more than two years from the point when the requester pulled your credit reports originally. Until then, the best thing that you can do is to avoid making requests for additional credit and loans.

Deleting of Medical Bills

Delinquent medical bills have a lower impact on your credit score than they used to in both the FICO 9 and VantageScoring 4.0 models. For older models though, they still rank alongside delinquent credit accounts in their negative impacts on scores. Getting these removed from your credit report will require the credit repair company to use the four step process we outlined earlier in this chapter.

As a recap, this involves the following:

1. Submit a Dispute of Inaccurate Information to the Three Credit Bureaus
2. Submit a Dispute of Incorrect Information to the Original Creditor
3. Make An Offer for a Pay for Delete Compromise
4. Request a Goodwill Deletion if You Have Already Repaid the Debt

With medical bills that are delinquent, you can also request that your credit repair company make an Offer for a Settlement for Delete. You may not have the money to pay off the entire debt, but in many cases the creditor will be willing to negotiate in exchange for a partial payment of the debt in one lump sum amount.

It costs them nothing to delete the derogatory information from your medical account and gets them money back that they would likely never again see otherwise.

Deleting of Charged Off Accounts

The original creditor is the party that your credit repair company will have to approach directly about getting a charged off account deleted. In many cases, if this debt was correctly reported, the only way to get it removed will be in an offer to Pay the account in full in exchange for a deletion of derogatory items.

Many creditors will recognize that this is the only way in which they will be able to recover on an account that they have already given up on entirely.

Credit repair companies have years of experience in handling these kinds of negotiations and know the right buttons to push to get it done.

Deleting of Tax Liens

Fortunately for millions of consumers in the U.S. today, the credit bureaus automatically took care of the deleting of all tax liens in the years of 2017 and 2018. There are no longer any liens of any kind, nor even any public or private judgments of any kind (except bankruptcies) shown on any of your credit reports today.

Key Takeaways from this Chapter

With 79 percent of all credit reports riddled with mistakes, it is entirely in your rights to have the big three credit bureaus prove the data or remove it entirely.

* * *

You could pay as little as $30 per month to one of these companies, but beware that you generally get what you pay for with credit repair (as well as in most areas of life).

* * *

Credit repair services are legal in every state of the U.S.

* * *

The easiest and fastest way to check out a credit repair company's legitimacy and all around reputation is to go to the Better Business Bureau website and enter their name.

* * *

It is always a good idea to go with one of the top credit repair companies to ensure that you get legitimate credit repair services at a fair price.

* * *

Credit repair companies have years of experience in handling negotiations and know the right buttons to push to get it done.

* * *

Legitimately listed hard inquiries on your credit reports can not be removed either by you or any credit repair organization.

. * * *

No matter how good a credit repair company may be, it is not possible for them to get a discharged bankruptcy removed from your credit files.

* * *

Lexington Law is something like the gold standard of traditional credit repair companies.

* * *

Credit Pros are the most expensive of the big five credit repair companies.

How to Keep Your Credit and Guard It

So by now you have followed the recommendations in this book and seen substantial improvements in your credit report along with accompanying resulting significant gains in your credit score. If this is you then well done but your work is not finished yet.

You will still need to make serious efforts to keep this good credit and defend it. There are many threats out there in cyberspace today against which you must guard your credit profile and score. We look at these in this the final chapter of the book.

Beware the Debt Snowball Effect

If you do not pay off your balance each month, then your creditor will gladly add interest to it. Each month in which you make charges that you do not pay completely down, your total balance will continue to grow until it snowballs out of control on you. At this point, you will likely have exceeded the FICO scoring model credit usability ratio limit of 30 percent that they want to see.

Then you will start to be penalized significantly in points for exceeding it on one or more revolving credit accounts and especially if your average ratio on all accounts surpasses 30 percent.

Guarding Your Credit – Using the Debt Snowball Method

If you have let your debt snowball out of control, then you will probably need to make use of an effective and proven method of paying it down like the Snowball Method. This method of liquidating debt was originally conceived of and made famous by personal finance guru and radio talk show host Dave Ramsey. According to this model, it is the momentum not the math that makes it easier to pay down your debt.

The way that you do this in practice is to list out all of your credit card debts according to the amount owed. You begin by first paying down your tiniest debt, then move up to the next smallest one, paying them off one by one. Keep moving up the credit card size ladder until they are all paid off. The key is that these early and easy to achieve small wins will not only build your confidence but will give the necessary momentum to attack the larger piles of debt towards the end.

It is the opposite of the debt avalanche model of attacking debt by paying down the highest interest rate accounts first, then moving down the interest rate credit card ladder until they are all paid down. While the Debt Snowball may be easier to follow, without a doubt the debt avalanche method saves you money in the long run and pays the debt off faster. The reason is because by paying down the card with the greatest interest rate later, you let it sit and continue accruing interest.

This means that you will pay back a small fortune in interest using the Debt Snowball method.

If you do opt to use the Debt Snowball method, your goal should be to pay not only the minimum monthly payment on this smallest balance account, but also an additional $100 per month. Then when you finish paying down the first debt, add the minimum monthly payment you were making to the hundred dollars and apply this towards the next smallest debt[80].

In every case, you should always make all minimum payments on all accounts during the process, or you will destroy your payment history on your credit report. Remember that this is the single most important category, and you should defend your timely monthly payment history with every breath in your body.

Handling Identity Theft Effectively

If you become a victim of identity theft, you will unfortunately be in nearly the majority with consumers in the United States today. In the last five years, around 48 percent of Americans have had their identities stolen, creating huge amounts of trouble and chaos in their lives.

Here are the seven steps which you should follow immediately to effectively handle becoming a victim of identity theft.

1. Immediately contact all impacted credit card banks and creditors

2. Set a fraud alert on your three credit reports

3. Pull your credit reports and check them for fraud – you should sign up for a free credit report service like Credit Karma or Discover It to allow you to check these as often as you feel necessary, at least on a monthly

basis for a while. This will not impact your credit score by creating soft inquiries only on your credit reports

4. Freeze Your Credit – you only have to contact one of the three credit reporting bureaus to have this done across the board

5. Report your identity theft and circumstances to the FTC – this is the federal government agency that handles investigation of identity theft in America today

6. File a police report – you may need this if you have to repair your credit reports as a result of the identity theft

7. Remove fraudulent information from your credit reports – Once you have checked over your credit reports, you may need to contact the big three credit bureaus to get any fraudulent information or accounts taken off of your profile. Thankfully the FTC has created a sample letter template that you can utilize in drafting your letter. Be sure to include copies of your police report and identification information with the fraudulent information detailed.

8. Be sure to change out all of your affected passwords

9. Replace your stolen Social Security Number if this was impacted

10. Contact your utility and phone companies[81] and make them aware of the identity theft as well[82].

Sample letter from the FTC reprinted below for your convenience:

Equifax
P.O. Box 105069
Atlanta, GA 30348-5069

-or-

Experian
P.O. Box 9554
Allen, TX 75013

-or-

TransUnion
Fraud Victim Assistance Department
P.O. Box 2000
Chester, PA 19016

[RE: Your Account Number (if known)]

Dear Sir or Madam:

I am a victim of identity theft. The information listed below, which appears on my credit report, does not relate to any transaction(s) that I have made. It is the result of identity theft.

[Identify item(s) resulting from the identity theft that should be blocked, by name of the source, such as the credit card issuer or bank, and type of item, such as credit account, checking account, etc.]

Please block this information from my credit report, pursuant to section 605B of the Fair Credit Reporting Act, and send the required notifications to all furnishers of this information.

Enclosed are the following:

A copy of my credit report I received from your company. The fraudulent items are circled.

A copy of my Identity Theft Report and proof of my identity.

A copy of section 605B of the Fair Credit Reporting Act, which requires you to block the fraudulent information on my credit report resulting from identity theft within four business days and to promptly notify the furnisher(s) of that information.

I appreciate your prompt attention to this matter, and await your reply.

Sincerely,
[Your Name]

Enclosures: [List what you are enclosing]

Identity Theft Report

Proof of identity: [a copy of my driver's license/other government-issued identification card/other]

Copy of Credit Report

How To Know If Your Identity Has Been Compromised

The good news is that there are some telltale warning signs that your identity has been compromised. Keep your eyes open for any of the following warning signs that you have been hacked somewhere:

1. There are inexplicable withdrawals from your bank account, or you find unknown charges on one or more of your credit cards

2. Your bills and other mail stop arriving

3. Merchants no longer accept your checks

4. Debt collectors start contacting you regarding debts that are not your own

5. Your credit report shows new accounts and/or charges that do not belong to you

6. Medical groups begin to bill you for treatments that you did not receive

7. You receive a notification from the IRS that they had more than one tax return filed in your name or that you received income from an employer for whom you never worked

8. You receive a notice that your personal information was hacked in an account breach via a firm where you have an account or with whom you do business

Steps to Take If Your Identity Has Been Stolen

There are five steps that you really should take immediately if you discover that your identity has been stolen. Do not wait to do these or the damage may become far worse than it already is.

1. Notify your banks and creditors
2. Put a freeze on your credit and a fraud alert on your credit reports
3. Report your stolen identity to the appropriate federal financial authority the FTC
4. Go to the police station and file a police report
5. Change all of your account passwords immediately[83]

These actions will at least stop the fraud from spreading and getting any worse. Thanks to the credit freeze, the identity thieves will be unsuccessful in opening any new credit accounts in your name. The fraud alert on your credit reports will act as a time stamp so that any suspicious activities in the future are easier to get removed.

A police report is further physical evidence that you have been hacked. By changing your passwords, you can keep the identity thieves from getting into your online account access.

7 Tips for Protecting Your Credit

Protecting your credit is a lifelong proactive task. Here are the seven steps that you should follow to help ensure that you do not suffer a loss of credit score points along the journey.

1. Keep Divorce From Destroying Your Credit

Divorce is unfortunately a reality for more than half of marriages in America today. There is no reason for this destruction of your marriage to also destroy your credit. Make certain that you personally make all monthly minimum payments and mortgage or car payments on any accounts which are in both of your names.

Never assume that you spouse will do this on his or her own, or even that they will live up to a verbal commitment or even a judge-imposed court order to do so. If one of you fails to make any payments, then both of your credit reports and scores will suffer the same fate.

2. Open an Emergency Bank Account

This should be the account that you only use when you have a bona fide emergency. This might include a car accident, devastating illness, loss of job or income, or other real emergency. Many Americans have overlooked or entirely neglected this critical step to have money available to continue paying their bills when disaster inevitably strikes (which is usually when you least expect it or are prepared for it too).

3. Always Check Your Monthly Statements

One of the quickest ways to spot identity theft is through taking the time to review your monthly statements. You may be busy and this is a hassle to do, but it is the surest ways to catch fraudulent activity on your credit card or bank accounts. If you see any suspicious activity that you did not authorize, then be sure to contact the appropriate merchant, bank, or creditor right away to mitigate the damage.

The creditors are responsible for reimbursing you for fraudulent activity, and banks too, but only if you report it in a timely fashion.

4. Do Not Put Confidential Information on Social Networking Sites Ever

You can not trust the social networking sites. Anyone at all (and not just friends) can access this personal information and use it to steal your identity. Many frauds have begun because of these social networking sites and people choosing to reveal intimate information that they simply should not. Stay safe by being smart, and keep all personal information confidential online.

5. Never Use Your Credit or Bank Debit Cards on an Unsecured Website

It is easy to check out the security of a website. Most browsers will tell you the status if you mouse your cursor over the address bar at the top of your screen. Unsecured websites are fraud and identity theft just waiting to happen. This is an easy problem that you can avoid with only a few seconds of caution online.

6. Create a New Credit File

Unfortunately, it is illegal for you to personally create a new credit file for yourself. The good news is that if you possess poor personal credit, you can start up a business and develop a separate business credit file which has no correlation to your personal credit file. All that is required is that you form a business, select a corporate structure, abide by the appropriate IRS requirements, and then finally establish a business line of credit. By keeping a healthy and timely credit profile for the business, you will be able to establish lines of credit and borrow money using the business credit file.

7. Keep Credit Cards and Contact Numbers Secure

Keep all of your credit card numbers and contact numbers in a secure place, separate from where you keep your credit cards themselves – you should have an action plan in the event that your wallet is physically stolen. This starts with having the associated account numbers and customer service contact phone numbers on all of your credit card accounts that you keep in your wallet somewhere separate and secure.

Should you be robbed, get on the phone and start cancelling these credit cards immediately. While you are on the phone with your creditors, you can request replacement cards and new pin numbers from them. If you do this in the immediate hours after you are robbed, then you will likely avoid having to deal with the hassle of fraudulent credit card charges later.

The Best Way to Deal With Bankruptcy

Sometimes events beyond your control (or mistakes that you made when you were younger and foolish) catch up with your credit and personal finances. At this point, it may actually be your best option to get a fresh start through filing for bankruptcy. The downside is that for the next several years, you will be a credit pariah. As you near the seven to 10 years when the bankruptcy falls off of your credit report though, lenders and creditors will once again start to approach you. They realize that you are unlikely to want to file bankruptcy again any time soon, and will be willing to give you another chance, albeit at much higher accompanying interest rates while you rebuild your shattered credit profile.

There is nothing that you can do to remove the derogatory remarks associated with bankruptcy from your credit report any sooner than the legal timeframe it must remain on there. You can double check that all of the information being reported to the big three credit bureaus (Experian, Equifax, and TransUnion) is at least correct.

Any accounts that were charged off can not continue to be reported as delinquent or sent out to collections. It is a good idea to send your letter of discharge to each of the three credit reporting bureaus so that they are intimately aware of what can and can not be reported on your personal credit file. Taking this proactive step is the easiest way to effectively manage your bankruptcy once it has been discharged.

Using Credit Counselling and Credit Protection Services

There may be times when you need to avail yourself of credit counselling services to help protect your credit. This is nothing to be ashamed of, it only means that you have gotten in over your head with your revolving carried debt. Attacking the problem head on is the best way to solve it. Remember that getting involved with credit counselling will not negatively impact your credit scores directly in any way.

What a solid credit counselling organization will first do is to offer you help with financial management and budgeting education. This will enable you to better regain control of your personal credit and debt so that you can get it in hand for the future.

The fact that you have availed yourself of such classes does not show up on your credit report in any way.

They may also offer you a service to help you repay your debt more efficiently called debt management plans. Repaying your debt this way will cause a note to be made on affected accounts, yet this does not affect your credit scores in any meaningful way. Debt management plans have the credit counselling agency negotiating deals for lower interest rates or even lower payments directly with your creditors and lenders.

This will cause a comment or note to be added on your accounts that they are being paid back via a credit counselling program or even a debt management plan. Lenders who are carefully reviewing your credit report would see this information if they are looking closely.

These notations do not affect your credit score in any way whatsoever[84].

Finding A Reputable Credit Counselling Service

(That Will Not Harm Your Credit Score)

If you find that you have started living from one pay check to the next, or have become worried about keeping to a budget, then you should start seeking out a good credit counsellor before you fall behind on your credit card bills and loan payments.

Credit counselling organizations of high repute are able to successfully advise you in managing your debts and your cash flow, assist you in creating a workable budget which you can actually stick to, and provide you with no cost workshops and other educational materials.

Their staff will be filled by highly trained and certified credit counsellors who are well versed in debt and money management, consumer credit issues, and budgeting matters. You can expect them to thoroughly review and talk over your whole financial situation with you as they help you create a specific plan to attack your money problems head on. These upfront counselling meetings commonly take an hour. They will always offer you follow up sessions to continue the discussions and review the working progress of your particular plan.

You will know a reputable credit counselling organization by the way that they offer you completely free information on themselves and their services without asking for you to give them any personal details or information on your scenario. Firms that will not do this are waving red flags. Look elsewhere for your help.

A number of military bases, universities, housing authorities, credit unions, and U.S. Cooperative Extensive Service branches will run not for profit credit counselling programs. Your bank or local consumer protection agency can also help to refer good outfits. After you obtain a list of counselling organizations that you can work with, you should run each name by your local consumer protection agency (like the BBB) and your state's Attorney General office.

They will know if other consumers have raised complaints about them.

Remember that just because no complaints have been filed does not guarantee their legitimacy. Fortunately, the U.S. Trustee Program maintains a list of reputable credit counselling organizations that are fully approved to deliver pre-bankruptcy counselling. You can rely on all of these organizations to be honest as they have been both thoroughly vetted and have proven themselves time and again.

Once you have completed your background due diligence, you should interview your final short list of candidates. The majority of reputable credit counselling organizations are actually not for profit outfits. This helps them to provide their service in person via local offices. Otherwise they can give you these services either over the phone or even online.

Be forewarned that not for profit status does not mean that all services will be affordable, free, or even legitimate. Some credit counselling outfits assess considerable fees. They might hide these. Others will ask (and even pressure) their customers to give so-called "voluntary" contributions. These can lead to still higher debt[85].

Protecting Your Credit Card From Identity Theft

Identity theft is an endemic problem in America today. If you have not become a victim of it yet, then you likely will in the next several years. A way around it is to employ one of the identity theft prevention services. The name brand in this department is Norton 360 Life Lock, though other competitors offer similar services.

Norton 360 Life Lock is an online and offline multi-layered protection service provided in real time against threats to your identity. This advanced level of security safeguards you against threats to information contained on your computers and your financial and personal information whether you are on the computer or off of it. This starts with their Life Lock Identity Alert System.

If your name, address, Social Security Number, or date of birth are used anywhere in an application for services or credit, you will be immediately notified.

It extends on to credit monitoring. The service keeps a close eye on your credit report via one of the leading big three credit bureaus. It will alert you if there is a significant change in an effort to detect any fraud that is underway early on.

To help you in the event that your identity is compromised or stolen, this service can include an impressive Million Dollar Protection. Any lost money or personal expenses in recovering your identity are covered by $25,000 per single incident and up to one million dollars if you need credit repair experts and lawyers to assist in restoring your compromised identity.

These services start from $8.99 per month and go on up to their highest tier of service at $25.99 per month. For this affordable price, you get the peace of mind in knowing that your identity is protected with an ironclad guarantee.

You can get more information on this service by going to their website at: https://us.norton.com/products/norton-360-lifelock-select

Protecting Your Credit from Student Loan Debt

Finally we turn our attention to an area that has become an epidemic – student loans and the inability of young individuals to ever repay them. The latest figures as of time of publication have student loans at over $1.4 trillion dollars and climbing. Many of these borrowers will fall behind on payments and eventually default entirely.

It can wreck your credit when these unpaid loans appear negatively on your credit reports. Be sure they will show up sooner or later if you default.

Though you may be seemingly hopelessly saddled with enormous ongoing student loan payments, there is some light at the end of the proverbial tunnel in the form of new and little known ways to limit your repayments.

These include extended repayment plans, graduated repayment plans, and Income Based Repayment plans with the Secret Student Loan Forgiveness Program.

With an extended repayment plan, the magic is that the federal government will kindly allow you to simply expand the amount of monthly payments you will make in the lifetime of your loan. This can be for as long as 25 years. All that it takes to accomplish is to contact your lender and tell them that you want to extend your repayment plan. By taking it out from the standard 10 to 25 years, you will massively reduce your payments on a $38,000 loan amount. Instead of paying back a crippling $381 per month, you will now repay at a rate of $196 per month, a dramatic monthly savings of $185 per month, or nearly half.

Using a graduated repayment plan, you can do even better than this. Again you will have 25 years to fully pay down your $38,000 in sample student loans, but they will build up the payments over time as you have more income to rely on in the repayments. Your initial payments would only amount to $120 per month in your first year. By the last year, you would be up to $359 per month in payments.

You could also do this on a shorter time frame using the original 10 year repayment plan, with initial payments amounting to $213 per month and rising to $638 per month in year nine. All that you have to do to get onto this advantageous repayment plan is to contact your lender and request it.

There is also a little known and highly useful third option called Income Based Repayment. In this generally self explanatory option, your payments will be calculated using your underlying income. The formula factors in your income amount, the poverty line in your state, and then sets your repayment amount at 15 percent of your remaining income (or 10 percent for new borrowers).

Another fantastic appeal of this Income Based Repayment is that you can get student loan forgiveness on any remaining debt from this loan after either 20 or 25 years, depending on the date in which your loans originated. This is sometimes referred to as the Secret Student Loan Forgiveness Program.

Consider that if you obtained your original student loans before the date of July 1, 2014, then your payment could amount to as little as $77 per month. For those who got their loans after July 1, 2014, the student loan repayment amount could drop to as little as only $52 per month[86].

Key Takeaways from this Chapter

You will pay back a small fortune in interest using the Debt Snowball method.

* * *

Put a freeze on your credit and a fraud alert on your credit reports.

* * *

Report your stolen identity to the appropriate federal financial authority the FTC.

* * *

The creditors are responsible for reimbursing you for fraudulent activity, and banks too, but only if you report it in a timely fashion.

* * *

Do Not Put Confidential Information on Social Networking Sites Ever.

* * *

Keep Credit Cards and Contact Numbers Secure.

* * *

Using a solid credit counselling organization will not affect your credit score in any way whatsoever.

* * *

A reputable credit counselling organization will offer you completely free information on themselves and their services without asking for you to give them any personal details or information on your scenario.

Resources and Bonuses

Extra Bonus - Free Financial Dictionary

The 100 Most Popular Financial Terms Explained

New 2020 updated edition with description for crypto-currency terms Bitcoin and Ethereum. This practical financial dictionary helps you understand and comprehend more than 100 most common financial terms. It was written with an emphasis to quickly grasp the context without using jargon.

With the alphabetical order, it makes it quick and easy to find what you are looking for.

This book is useful if you are new to business and finance. It includes over 100 most popular financial terms for the business owner, investors, and entrepreneurs. It also covers the lingo that was introduced in the financial crisis of 2008.

Every financial term is explained in detail and includes also examples. It is based on common usage as practiced by financial professionals.

Download your free edition from Amazon:

bit.ly/free-dictionary

Please Leave Your Review on Amazon

I hope that the information in this book exceeded your expectations. I would very much appreciate it if you would please take a few minutes today or over the next few days to share your experience on Amazon. This feedback helps me improve my ability to provide you with the best credit information possible.

If you have found valuable information in this book, please give it a solid 5-star review on Amazon. In case you do not feel it deserves that, please do not post any feedback yet! Email me instead with your feedback. I am reading all feedback comments, and I ensure you that I will make every effort to address your concerns in my reply. Please go to this address:

bit.ly/high-credit

Thomas Herold - Amazon Author Page
amazon.com/author/thomasherold

You can also go to amazon.com and simply search for ‚Thomas Herold‘. Then scroll until you find ‚High Credit Score Secrets‘.

Visit The Author's Websites

Find additional information and updated news about anything related to credit cards, credit score and credit report. If you still have questions that are not addressed in this book, please ask the author and you will usually get an answer in less than 24 hours.

Website: highcreditscoresecrets.com

The Money Deception

Major financial changes are coming in 2020 – are you prepared? In this explosive book 'The Money Deception', I provide the most sophisticated insight, and shocking details about the current monetary system. Never before has the massive manipulation of money caused so much despair and economic inequality all over the world. Reads like fiction but it's as real as it gets!

Website: moneydeception.com

Herold's Financial Dictionary

The most comprehensive financial dictionary on the Internet with over 1000 financial terms explained. Every terms is explained in clear and concise article style description with practical examples.

Website: financial-dictionary.info

Herold's Financial IQ Book Series

This new financial series includes 16 titles, covering every aspect and category of the financial market. Starting with Personal Finance, Real Estate and Banking term. Covering Corporate Finance, Investment as well as Economics.

It also includes Retirement, Trading, and Accounting terms. In addition, you'll find Debt, Bankruptcy, Mortgage, Small Business, and Wall Street terminology explained. Not to forget Laws & Regulations as well as important acronyms and abbreviations.

All books from this series are available in Kindle, Paperback and Audio edition.

Website - Financial Education Is Your Best Investment
financial-dictionary.com

The Money Deception

The Money Deception - What Banks & Governments Don't Want You to Know

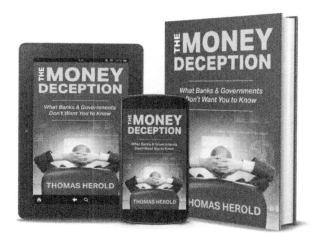

„It is well enough that people of the nation do not understand our banking and monetary system, for if they did, I believe there would be a revolution before tomorrow morning." - Henry Ford

In this new startling book, Mr. Herold provides the most sophisticated insight and shocking details about the current monetary system. Never before has the massive manipulation of money caused so much despair and income inequality all over the world.

Reader Discretion Advised

If you are not prepared to face the facts and the shocking truth of our global financial system, it is advisable not to read "The Money Deception". It's about the world's most powerful and influential system. Not only that the foundations of what you believed about money might be shaken up, but the book may also stir emotions and challenge the intellect.

Up to 90% of Your Income Is Seized - Why Do You Let This Happen?

This book unveils over 20 secret methods that banks, governments, and corporations are using to legally strip up to 90% of your income. It reveals the striking facts:

- Why the current monetary system stands before the abyss
- The magic trick how banks create money out of thin air
- The myth of GDP growth and what really causes it
- The physiological methods by which advertisers and insurances get your money
- Will the government soon be forced to support Universal Basic Income?
- Why crypto-currencies could free us from central banks and government regulations
- Why a resource based economy could be the solution and make money obsolete
- What you can do right now to shift from a money mindset to wealth creation

Over 8 years in the making...

The stunning details about the biggest fraud in history ever – happening to you right now.

Bubbles blow – in 2000 the Internet business bubble imploded, only eight years later the housing market crashed. Now we have the everything bubble!

More than 3 trillion dollars – that's a three with 12 zeros – have been injected into the market since then to keep it from collapsing.

The Catastrophic Results of Money Manipulation

This money has been souped up by the 1% that now control 50% of the world's wealth. The fastest and biggest wealth transfer in history is underway. Money evaporates from the middle class, leaving them struggling and without hope for retirement. The elite class is celebrating their biggest heist with insane, astronomical profits. This is not going to last.

The 'Everything Bubble' is Going to Bust

Understand the secret methods almost all banks and governments have been using - and still using today - to steal your money legally. It exposes in detail, brilliance and with clarity over 20 stunning tactics, which leaves you wondering why the whole system hasn't crashed a long time ago.

Brilliantly written and astoundingly easy to understand, this book is an eye-popping exposure of the most sophisticated fraud in the history of mankind. This is a must read if you want to survive the global monetary transformation that's underway right now.

What's Happening to Your Money?

Going all the way down into the rabbit hole, it shows you the root of the problem and also lays the foundation for the future. It describes the most likely transition into a new worldwide crypto-based currency, which will become the new basis of our financial system.

This new area marks one of the most significant changes in the history of money and has the potential to end the control of central banks and governments.

Available on Amazon as Kindle, Paperback and Audio Edition
bit.ly/money-deception

Herold Financial IQ Series

Financial Education Is Your Best Investment

Get Smart with the Financial IQ Series

The Herold Financial IQ series covers all major areas and aspects in the financial world. Starting with Personal Finance, Real Estate and Banking term. Covering Corporate Finance, Investment as well as Economics.

Also includes Retirement, Trading, and Accounting terms. In addition, you'll find Debt, Bankruptcy, Mortgage, Small Business, and Wall Street terminology explained. Not to forget Laws & Regulations as well as important acronyms and abbreviations.

See an overview of all titles on Amazon below:

bit.ly/herold-financial-iq

Herold Financial IQ Series - All Editions

All books of this series are available in Kindle, Paperback and Audio edition.

  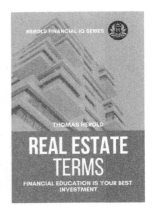

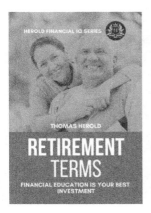

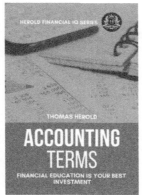

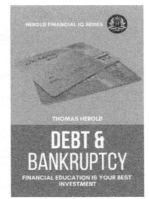

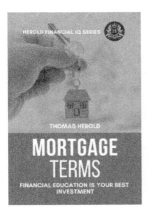

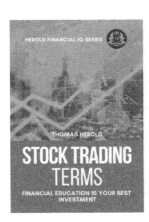

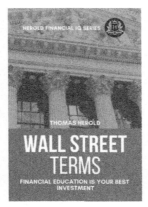

Bibliography

[1] https://www.credit.com/tools/lifetime-cost-of-debt/

[2] https://www.westerracu.com/loans/home-loans/first-mortgage-loan/first-time-homebuyer-product/mortgage-payment-examples

[3] https://www.debt.org/credit/report/scoring-models/

[4] https://www.myfico.com/credit-education/fico-scores-vs-credit-scores

[5] https://www.debt.com/credit-faq/how-does-leasing-a-car-affect-your-credit-score/

[6] https://www.investopedia.com/mortgage/refinance/my-fico-score/

[7] https://www.experian.com/blogs/ask-experian/tax-liens-are-no-longer-a-part-of-credit-reports/

[8] https://www.valuepenguin.com/average-credit-score

[9] https://www.creditdonkey.com/credit-score-statistics.html

[10] https://www.valuepenguin.com/average-credit-score#average-credit-score-score-by-age

[11] https://www.valuepenguin.com/average-credit-score#nogo

[12] https://www.thebalance.com/closure-inactive-credit-cards-961069

[13] https://www.thebalance.com/remove-credit-report-late-payments-4134208).

[14] https://www.creditdonkey.com/credit-card-fraud-statistics.html

[15] https://www.experian.co.uk/consumer/guides/electoral-roll.html

[16] https://www.debt.com/credit-faq/do-tax-liens-affect-my-credit-score/

[17] https://www.experian.com/blogs/ask-experian/judgments-no-longer-included-on-credit-report/

[18] https://www.creditkarma.com/advice/i/accounts-in-collections/

[19] https://www.thebalance.com/does-foreclosure-or-short-sale-affect-credit-score-2388736

[20] https://www.nerdwallet.com/blog/finance/late-bill-payment-reported/

21 https://www.thebalance.com/how-your-debt-affects-your-credit-score-960489

22 https://www.creditkarma.com/auto/i/car-repossession-hurt-credit/

23 https://thescore.vantagescore.com/article/266/avoid-derogatory-narratives-your-credit-reports

24 https://www.experian.com/blogs/ask-experian/credit-education/report-basics/how-and-when-collections-are-removed-from-a-credit-report/

25 https://www.creditkarma.com/advice/i/age-credit-history-affect-credit-scores/

26 https://www.experian.co.uk/consumer/loans/guides/payday-loans.html

27 https://www.experian.com/blogs/ask-experian/does-being-unemployed-hurt-your-credit-scores/

28 https://www.experian.com/blogs/ask-experian/what-is-a-cash-advance/

29 https://www.nerdwallet.com/blog/finance/does-closing-a-credit-card-hurt-credit-score/

30 https://www.thebalance.com/can-i-close-a-credit-card-with-a-balance-960151

31 https://www.consumerfinance.gov/ask-cfpb/what-is-a-credit-report-en-309/

32 https://www.nerdwallet.com/blog/finance/read-credit-report/

33 https://www.creditkarma.com/credit-cards/i/three-credit-bureaus/

34 https://www.creditkarma.com/credit-cards/i/how-types-credit-affect-score/

35 https://www.thebalance.com/why-you-should-check-your-credit-score-regularly-4083165

36 https://www.myfico.com/credit-education/whats-in-my-credit-report

37 https://www.discover.com/credit-cards/resources/things-to-consider-when-choosing-a-credit-card/

38 https://www.thebalance.com/credit-score-myths-960522

39 https://www.creditkarma.com/credit-cards/i/credit-card-types-to-consider/

40 https://www.thebalance.com/ways-to-build-good-credit-960109

41 https://www.fool.com/the-ascent/credit-cards/articles/how-to-achieve-a-perfect-credit-score/

42 https://www.nerdwallet.com/blog/finance/30-percent-credit-utilization-ratio-rule/

43 https://www.businessinsider.com/strategies-to-pay-off-credit-card-debt-fast

44 https://www.thebalance.com/best-first-time-credit-cards-4767778

45 https://www.creditkarma.com/credit-cards/i/best-first-credit-card-for-young-adults/

46 https://www.creditkarma.com/credit-cards/i/best-credit-cards-for-new-parents/

47 https://www.cardrates.com/advice/credit-cards-for-low-income/

48 https://www.nerdwallet.com/best/credit-cards/premium

49 https://www.thebalance.com/best-credit-cards-for-small-business-owners-4767793

50 https://www.nerdwallet.com/blog/credit-cards/best-credit-card-offers-for-retirees/

51 https://www.nerdwallet.com/blog/finance/fair-debt-collection-practices-act

52 https://www.investopedia.com/terms/f/fair-credit-billing-act-fcba.asp

53 https://www.debt.org/credit/your-consumer-rights/truth-lending-act/

54 http://www.bcsalliance.com/credit-report-consumer-statement.html

55 https://www.experian.com/blogs/ask-experian/what-is-a-609-dispute-letter/

56 https://www.thebalance.com/how-to-fix-credit-after-identity-theft-1947660

57 https://www.thebalance.com/recognize-debt-collection-scams-4142803

58 https://www.crediful.com/late-payments/#ixzz64xTBq0iV

59 https://www.creditkarma.com/advice/i/how-to-remove-medical-collections-from-credit-reports/

60 https://www.thebalance.com/how-to-repair-your-credit-960377

61 https://www.creditkarma.com/advice/i/credit-repair-companies/

62 https://www.thebalance.com/how-to-repair-your-credit-960377

63 https://www.thebalance.com/how-to-repair-your-credit-960377

64 https://www.investopedia.com/terms/c/credit-repair-organizations-act-croa.asp

65 https://www.myfico.com/credit-education/credit-reports/sample-credit-report-dispute-letter-of-explanation

66 https://imaxcredit.com/credit-dispute-letters-credit-bureau/#The_credit_bureau_dispute_letter

67 https://www.consumer.ftc.gov/articles/0384-sample-letter-disputing-errors-your-credit-report

68 https://www.experian.com/blogs/ask-experian/what-is-a-609-dispute-letter/

69 https://www.thebalance.com/how-to-repair-credit-after-bankruptcy-960380

70 https://www.crediful.com/foreclosures/#ixzz659C0swHM

71 https://www.fool.com/calculators/should-i-consolidate-my-loans.aspx

72 https://www.nerdwallet.com/blog/banking/blacklisted-by-chexsystems-what-to-know/

73 https://www.insurance.wa.gov/clue-comprehensive-loss-underwriting-exchange

74 https://www.consumer.ftc.gov/articles/0220-utility-services

75 https://www.experian.com/blogs/ask-experian/can-remove-negative-accurate-information-credit-report/

76 https://www.nerdwallet.com/blog/finance/credit-repair/

77 https://www.creditkarma.com/advice/i/credit-repair-companies/

78 https://www.debt.com/credit-repair/law/

79 https://www.thebalance.com/remove-negative-credit-report-960734

80 https://www.debt.org/advice/debt-snowball-method-how-it-works

81 https://www.bankrate.com/finance/credit/steps-for-victims-of-identity-fraud.aspx

82 https://www.identitytheft.gov/Sample-Letters/identity-theft-credit-bureau

83 https://www.consumer.ftc.gov/articles/0271-warning-signs-identity-theft

84 https://www.experian.com/blogs/ask-experian/the-impact-of-credit-counseling-on-credit-scores

85 https://www.consumer.ftc.gov/articles/0153-choosing-credit-counselor

86 https://thecollegeinvestor.com/18246/5-legal-ways-to-lower-your-student-loan-payment